CHARLES DICKENS

Charles Dickens was born in Port
Wellington House Academy and \
stenographer and shorthand report   ... ...s first
collection of pieces, *Sketches by Boz* (1836).

His major works include *The Pickwick Papers* (1836), *Oliver
Twist* (1837–9), *Nicholas Nickleby* (1838–9), *A Christmas Carol*
(1843), *Martin Chuzzlewit* (1843–4), *David Copperfield* (1849–
50), *Bleak House* (1852–3), *Hard Times* (1854), *Little Dorrit*
(1855–7), *A Tale of Two Cities* (1859), *Great Expectations*
(1860–1), *Our Mutual Friend* (1864–5) and the unfinished *The
Mystery of Edwin Drood* (1870), as well as other novels, books
and short stories. None of his major works has ever gone out of
print.

Dickens married Catherine Hogarth in 1836 and had ten
children with her. He died in June 1870 from a stroke and,
contrary to his wish to be buried in Rochester Cathedral, was
buried in Poets' Corner of Westminster Abbey.

ALASTAIR CORDING

Born and raised in Glasgow, Alastair Cording researched
Scottish theatre history for his PhD, subsequently lecturing at
Glasgow and Strathclyde Universities. His extensive career as an
actor and director led to writing, as the result of the Edinburgh
Fringe First-winning epic, *The Golden City*.

He has written for a number of theatre companies: a series of
children's plays for Masque; *Mrs O's Saturday Nights* (Covent
Garden Festival); *Fatale* (Basingstoke Haymarket); and *The
Walshingham Organ*, *Margaret Catchpole* and *Margaret Down
Under* (Eastern Angles).

Adapted works include Wilkie Collins's *No Name* for Eastern
Angles; *Wild Harbour* and *Gay Hunter* for BBC Radio; Alasdair
Gray's *Lanark,* and Lewis Grassic Gibbon's *Scots Quair* trilogy
(*Sunset Song, Cloud Howe* and *Grey Granite)* for TAG.

Other Adaptations in this Series

AFTER MRS ROCHESTER
Polly Teale
Based on the life and work
of Jean Rhys

ANIMAL FARM
Ian Wooldridge
Adapted from George Orwell

ANNA KARENINA
Helen Edmundson
Adapted from Leo Tolstoy

ARABIAN NIGHTS
Dominic Cooke

BEAUTY AND THE BEAST
Laurence Boswell

BRONTË
Polly Teale
Based on the life and work
of the Brontës

THE CANTERBURY TALES
Mike Poulton
Adapted from Geoffrey Chaucer

A CHRISTMAS CAROL
Karen Louise Hebden
Adapted from Charles Dickens

CINDERELLA
Stuart Paterson

CORAM BOY
Helen Edmundson
Adapted from Jamila Gavin

DR JEKYLL AND MR HYDE
David Edgar
Adapted from Robert Louis Stevenson

EMMA
Martin Millar and Doon MacKichan
Adapted from Jane Austen

GONE TO EARTH
Helen Edmundson
Adapted from Mary Webb

GREAT EXPECTATIONS
Nick Ormerod and Declan Donnellan
Adapted from Charles Dickens

HANSEL AND GRETEL
Stuart Paterson

HIS DARK MATERIALS
Nicholas Wright
Adapted from Philip Pullman

JANE EYRE
Polly Teale
Adapted from Charlotte Brontë

THE JUNGLE BOOK
Stuart Paterson
Adapted from Rudyard Kipling

KENSUKE'S KINGDOM
Stuart Paterson
Adapted from Michael Morpurgo

KES
Lawrence Till
Adapted from Barry Hines

MADAME BOVARY
Fay Weldon
Adapted from Gustave Flaubert

MARY BARTON
Rona Munro
Adapted from Elizabeth Gaskell

THE MILL ON THE FLOSS
Helen Edmundson
Adapted from George Eliot

NORTHANGER ABBEY
Tim Luscombe
Adapted from Jane Austen

SLEEPING BEAUTY
Rufus Norris

SUNSET SONG
Alastair Cording
Adapted from
    Lewis Grassic Gibbon

TREASURE ISLAND
Stuart Paterson
Adapted from Robert Louis Stevenson

WAR AND PEACE
Helen Edmundson
Adapted from Leo Tolstoy

DAVID
COPPERFIELD

adapted from Charles Dickens's novel by

Alastair Cording

NICK HERN BOOKS

London

www.nickhernbooks.co.uk

A Nick Hern Book

This adaptation of *David Copperfield* first published in Great Britain as a paperback original in 2009 by Nick Hern Books Limited, 14 Larden Road, London W3 7ST

This adaptation of *David Copperfield* copyright © 2009 Alastair Cording

Alastair Cording has asserted his right to be identified as the author of this work

Cover image: Susanna Northern as Young David in the 2003 Eastern Angles production of *David Copperfield*. Photo by Mike Kwasniak. www.mikekwasniak.co.uk

Cover design: Ned Hoste, 2H

Typeset by Nick Hern Books, London

Printed and bound in Great Britain by CPI Antony Rowe, Chippenham, Wiltshire.

A CIP catalogue record for this book is available from the British Library

ISBN   978 1 84842 022 9

FSC
Mixed Sources
Product group from well-managed
forests and other controlled sources
Cert no. SGS-COC-2953
www.fsc.org
© 1996 Forest Stewardship Council

The Adaptation and the Novel

David Copperfield is, at its core, about the exploration of couples and marriages, about the effects on adult life of childhood experience, and about Dickens's consideration of the model for the perfect woman. It is also a plea for kindness and tolerance, and a condemnation of the twin vices of over-indulgence and self-righteous cruelty.

As David's story unfolds, we are presented with a series of marriages and parent-child relationships. These range from the merciless rectitude of Murdstone's marriage to David's mother, the comic youthful folly of an inexperienced romantic young couple in David and Dora, the mutually supportive, platonic relationship of Betsey Trotwood and Mr Dick, the ruin of Emily's life by Steerforth's seduction, and the threatened nightmare of Agnes's acceptance of Uriah Heep, to the final mature perfection of David's love for Agnes. Throughout the tale is woven a repeated image of intense affection, in the gloriously eccentric Micawbers. Their chaotic life is redeemed by their unquestioning faith, trust, love, and – above all – respect, for each other. It is significant that the great crisis of the story – the final defeat of Uriah Heep – is provoked by the momentary breakdown of the Micawbers' intimacy.

In contrast to the series of marriages and pairings is the linear development of the theme of childhood influence. In this, David's ultimate survival of the horrors of Murdstone's ruthlessness, the casual cruelty of Creakle's ghastly school, and the mind-numbing drudgery of the bottle factory – is set against the destructive results of indulgence. Emily, Dora and Steerforth are each in some way disabled by a doting parent. The survival of David's humanity is also compared to the development in Uriah Heep of a monstrous self-righteousness founded on an upbringing of harsh hypocrisy.

There are also the women in David's life: the flawed perfection
of his fragile mother, too innocent and too trustful; the defiant
common sense and instinctive protectiveness of Clara Peggotty;
the lively flirtatiousness of Little Emily, which betrays her into
the romantic illusion of becoming a great lady; Aunt Betsey's
fierce independence; Dora's cheerful innocence and inability to
survive in a world uncushioned by her doting father's misguided
extravagance; the dignity and grandeur of Mrs Steerforth,
twisted, by bitter disappointment in her son, into a vindictiveness
against her son's victim; and lastly Agnes, a long-suffering, self-
sacrificing, intelligent, sweet-natured heroine whose love is
recognised and won by David only after he has been tested to the
limit by a life of hard knocks and cruel misfortunes.

Behind all is the social fabric of Victorian England, and
Dickens's striking vision of its vices, virtues and inequalities.
These are symbolised in the story's physical movement between
the dark, confusing Babel of London, the vast-skyed, watery
openness of East Anglia, and the Peggotty's boat-house, halfway between the stultifying repetition of ordered getting and
spending on the land, and the dangerous freedoms of the sea.
The boat-house, which seems such a solid home at the start, is
by the end a physical image of desolation and betrayal, just as
the aristocratic hauteur and charm of Steerforth and his mother
are transformed into images of moral desolation and betrayal.

Given the considerable scale of the novel, and Dickens's
unhesitating deployment of a regiment of minor characters,
incidents and observations, this stage adaptation has
concentrated on the essentials of David Copperfield's story,
endeavouring to maintain the colour, humour and drama of the
book, while creating a strong theatrical entertainment. It is
intended that a fluid, non-naturalistic style of presentation, and
an intelligent use of doubling in the casting of the play, will
underscore, contrast and draw comparisons to good effect; to
take the fullest advantage of specifically theatrical effects and
devices, rather than to be embarrassed by them.

As a result, much of the narrative in this version of *David
Copperfield* is given to Peggotty and Agnes, as a means of

establishing their intimacy with David, and of their significant involvement in his life. Some characters have vanished for the sake of dramatic clarity and some consolidated – most conspicuously Rosa Dartle and Mrs Steerforth. The Micawbers' flamboyance has been indulged by a deliberately 'operatic' approach to their exchanges, to contrast their comic liveliness with the drudgery of David's life, and with the deadening notions of respectability and moral rectitude. The order of certain incidents has also occasionally been changed, in particular the great storm which drowns Steerforth and Ham. This now comes after the emigration of the Peggottys and the Micawbers, to emphasise David's loneliness as all the connections to his past life disappear. It also permits a properly theatrical response to such a melodramatic set-piece.

The aim throughout has been to translate *David Copperfield* for the theatre; to create an exciting, fast-paced, clear and engaging stage play, recreating the great concerns of a great novel.

Production Notes

There are twenty-four named parts in all, thirteen male and eleven female, most of them substantial character roles.

Young David should be played by an actress.

The staging can be extremely simple: Ivan Cutting's original production for Eastern Angles Theatre Company made use of a brass double-bedstead which transformed into a huge variety of central props and settings: a horse-drawn cart, Peggotty's cramped boat-house, a schoolroom row of desks, a ship under sail, and was even when required a double bed. The stage directions follow the progress of the bed; other design solutions are of course possible.

Alastair Cording

Alastair Cording's adaptation of *David Copperfield* was first performed by Eastern Angles Theatre Company at the Wolsey Theatre, Ipswich, on 12 September 1995, before touring. The cast was as follows:

CREAKLE / DANIEL PEGGOTTY / MR DICK	Sean Buckley
YOUNG DAVID / AGNES	Siobhánn Carolan
DORA / EMILY / MOTHER	Kirsten Clark
STEERFORTH / URIAH HEEP	Toby Davies
DAVID COPPERFIELD / TRADDLES	Mark Feakins
BETSEY TROTWOOD / JANE MURDSTONE	Janet Jefferies
MURDSTONE / MICAWBER / HAM	Sévan Stephan
PEGGOTTY / MRS STEERFORTH / MRS MICAWBER	Claire Vousden

Director	Ivan Cutting
Designer	Fred Meller
Lighting Designer	Geoff Spain

The production was revived by Eastern Angles at the Wolsey Theatre, Ipswich, on 2 April 2003, before touring. There were the following changes to the cast and creative team:

YOUNG DAVID / AGNES	Susanna Northern
DORA / EMILY / MOTHER	Emma Jerrold
STEERFORTH / URIAH HEEP	Graham O'Mara
DAVID COPPERFIELD / TRADDLES	Carl Prekopp
MURDSTONE / MICAWBER / HAM	Jon Atkins

Lighting Designer	Peter Higton

Characters

YOUNG DAVID COPPERFIELD
DAVID COPPERFIELD

PEGGOTTY, *David's nurse and caretaker, Clara Peggotty*
DANIEL PEGGOTTY, *Peggotty's brother*
HAM, *Peggotty and Daniel's nephew*
EMILY, *Peggotty and Daniel's niece*

BETSEY TROTWOOD, *David's aunt*
MOTHER, *David's mother, Clara Copperfield*
EDWARD MURDSTONE, *David's stepfather*
JANE MURDSTONE, *Murdstone's sister*

CREAKLE, *headmaster of Salem House School*
TOMMY TRADDLES, *a schoolboy at Salem House*
JAMES STEERFORTH, *David's schoolfriend*

WILKINS MICAWBER, *David's landlord and friend*
MRS MICAWBER, *Micawber's wife*

DICK, *Richard Babley, Betsey's companion*
AGNES WICKFIELD, *daughter of Betsey's lawyer,*
    David's confidante
DORA SPENLOW, *daughter of one of David's employers,*
    David's first wife
MRS STEERFORTH, *Steerforth's mother*
URIAH HEEP, *a clerk*

BARKIS, *a coachman*
MICK, *a factory worker*
MEALY, *a factory worker*
MARY ANNE PARAGON, *a servant*

Plus a DOCTOR, *a* GANG OF CREDITORS, *a* THIEF, *a*
PAWNBROKER, *a* SOLDIER, SAILORS, *and various other*
MEN, WOMEN, GIRLS *and* BOYS.

ACT ONE

Scene One

In the centre of the stage stands a brass bed loaded with luggage. The COMPANY *swarm over it, hold a tableau, then go, leaving a carter –* BARKIS *– asleep with his back to us, and* YOUNG DAVID *and* PEGGOTTY, *half-asleep.* PEGGOTTY *pokes* BARKIS *awake.*

BARKIS. Whoa.

PEGGOTTY. Master Davy.

> PEGGOTTY *and* YOUNG DAVID *get off. Enter* HAM. *The bed is pushed offstage to be transformed into the boat-house.* YOUNG DAVID *and* PEGGOTTY *gaze around.* HAM *picks up their luggage.*

> Ham? Ham – there's a bag still to come off the cart. What does that driver-man Barkis think he's about? Still awake, Master Davy? This is Ham, my brother Daniel's boy. Ham? This is young Master David Copperfield, my very own Master Davy. Honest, Ham, it's like we've been on the road for ever, there were so many things delivered on the way. Up lanes and down lanes – parcels and packets and even a bedstead for some tavern – and Barkis had no conversation beyond whistling to himself and snoozing. It's as well the horse knew the Yarmouth road: you'd never have believed one man could have snored so much. Ah, Master Davy, my love, smell that air. Fish and pitch and oakum and tar and sea salt – and sailors! Proud I am to call myself a Yarmouth Bloater, for no one could doubt but Yarmouth is the finest place in the whole universe.

YOUNG DAVID. It's awfully flat, Peggotty! And the land and the sea are all mixed up. Look! There's a big black boat sailing on the ground over there!

HAM. Yon big black boat is our house, Master Davy.

YOUNG DAVID. Your house?

HAM. Aye, our house. She were a real boat once, Master Davy, and sailed the sea a thousand times, but now she has a roof and a door and windows in her sides –

PEGGOTTY. Tables and chairs and chests inside, and a clock and a painting of a lady with a parasol – everything just like in a proper house, but all snug and trim and cosy –

HAM. Just like a ship on the sea.

Enter DANIEL PEGGOTTY *and* EMILY.

DANIEL. Mr Davy, sir! Glad to see you. You'll find us rough, sir, but you'll find us ready. Say 'hello', Emily.

EMILY. Hello.

YOUNG DAVID. How do you do, Mr Peggotty. I am sure I shall be happy in such a wonderful house.

DANIEL. And how's your ma, sir? Did you leave her pretty jolly?

PEGGOTTY. That we did, Dan. As jolly as may be.

DANIEL. Well, Master Davy, if you can make out here for a fortnight, we shall be proud of your company.

HAM. Come on, Master Davy, we'll stow your gear, and Emily and me will show you around.

YOUNG DAVID, HAM *and* EMILY *go*.

DANIEL. Well, sister, you are with us again. (*They embrace.*) Never fear for the little lad. We'll give him two weeks of sea air, good cheer and good plain vittles, and send him home with colour in his cheeks. And we'll not be a-worrying beyond those two weeks, will we?

PEGGOTTY. No, Dan, you're right, we won't. There'll be time aplenty for worrying, after. My, but it's a treat to see you.

DANIEL. Little Emily seemed to think it a treat to see our Master Davy. Fair smitten with him, I thought.

PEGGOTTY. Are you turned matchmaker, then? I'll maybe soon be asking you to land me a catch. Barkis the carter is always a-grinning and a-nudging, and a-mumbling he's 'willin''. 'Barkis is willin'.' But willin' to what, he never do say.

YOUNG DAVID *returns.* EMILY *hovers in the background.*

DANIEL. Well, Master Davy, I bet you never thought you'd be a-staying aboard Noah's Ark!

YOUNG DAVID. Is that why you call your son 'Ham', then, because you live in an Ark?

DANIEL. Lord, no. His father gave it him.

YOUNG DAVID. I thought you were his father.

DANIEL. Bless you, no, sir. His father was my drowndead brother Joe.

YOUNG DAVID. But Emily's your daughter?

DANIEL. No, my brother-in-law Tom was her father.

YOUNG DAVID. Drowndead, Mr Peggotty?

DANIEL. Drowndead, Master Davy. And her mother passed on afore that.

PEGGOTTY. Mr Peggotty adopted Emily and Ham, Davy, so they be not left poor orphans. And him but a poor man himself, but a man as good as gold and true as steel –

DANIEL. No more of that. I do only what the next man would do. Do you run along with Emily, Master Davy, and see the sights of Yarmouth. Emily! Take this young gentleman and show him the ocean!

PEGGOTTY, DANIEL *and* HAM *go into the boat-house.* EMILY *and* YOUNG DAVID *join hands and run forward as if onto the seashore.*

Scene Two

YOUNG DAVID. Mr Peggotty is very good.

EMILY. Uncle Dan? Yes, he is good. He is the best man in the world. If I was ever to be a lady, I'd give him a sky-blue coat with diamond buttons, nankeen trousers, a red-velvet waistcoat, a cocked hat, a large gold watch, a silver pipe, and a box of money.

YOUNG DAVID. Would you like to be a lady?

EMILY. Yes. Of course. We should all be gentlefolks then. You and me, and Uncle, and Ham and Aunt Peggotty. We wouldn't mind then, when there come stormy weather – not for our own sakes, anyhow. We would for the poor fishermen's, to be sure, and we'd help 'em with money when they come to any hurt.

YOUNG DAVID. I'll marry you and make you a lady.

EMILY. You must ask my Uncle Dan, then. I know he's not my real father, but he's my adopted dad, so he can say yes when you ask for my hand.

PEGGOTTY *returns and gazes fondly at the two children playing.*

PEGGOTTY (*to DANIEL*). Like two young mavishes. They love each other as true and tender and pure and innocent as the best love there is.

DANIEL (*looks to the sea*). Tide's full in. Soon be time for the ebb.

Scene Three

The bed as boat-house is pushed forward with PEGGOTTY *and*
DANIEL *sat on the side, and the* CHILDREN *poking out from*
underneath. YOUNG DAVID *is in the bosom of the family,*
beside EMILY. DANIEL *finishes a jolly sea song.*

DANIEL (*sings*).
> Then up jumped the herring, the king of the sea,
> And said to the skipper, you'll never catch me,
> In this windy old weather, boys, stormy old weather, boys,
> When the wind blows we'll all pull together.

PEGGOTTY. Young Master David was born on a Friday night
like this. The clock began to strike twelve, and he began to
cry, simultaneous. Some folks say that babes born of that day
and hour are unlucky, and have the gift to see ghosts.

HAM. Lord, Davy, do you be seeing ghosts?

YOUNG DAVID. No, Ham, never.

PEGGOTTY. And you never were born to be unlucky, either,
that I'll warrant. Young Master Davy's poor father died six
months before he were born, so that, from the first, Davy, you
were born to be a blessing and a comfort to your dear mother.

DANIEL. And who could think it otherwise?

PEGGOTTY. No one! Save perhaps one, and that for the daftest
and maddest of causes.

HAM. Mad it must be, for anyone to take agin our Davy!

PEGGOTTY. An aunt of Davy's father, Miss Betsey Trotwood
by name, got herself wed to a husband younger than herself,
who was very handsome.

DANIEL. Handsome is as handsome does, I say.

PEGGOTTY. Just so, Dan. 'Twas said he beat Miss Betsey
Trotwood, and threatened her, till she could stand it no
longer, and paid him off to go to India, where he went wild

and rode about on elephants and baboons till he was dead.
Miss Betsey was so grieved by this news she bought a
seaside cottage near Dover, and retired. Davy's father had
been a great favourite of hers, but she had took against
marrying, and refused to visit. Until, that is, the afternoon of
a particular Friday.

Enter BETSEY TROTWOOD. YOUNG DAVID*'s birth will
be acted out.*

BETSEY. Is this the house? 'The Rookery'? David Copperfield
— what were you thinking of? Calling this house of yours
'The Rookery'! What folly! And worse folly, to get yourself
married! Married, indeed. And more folly to get yourself
married to a wax doll half your age, and to father a child, and
then to die! Folly, nothing but folly! Oh, David Copperfield —
what were you thinking of?

Enter MOTHER *and* PEGGOTTY, *with a saucepan
billowing smoke.*

MOTHER (*in despair*). Oooh, Peggotty!

BETSEY. Mrs David Copperfield? I am your late husband's
aunt.

MOTHER. Oh, yes — Miss Trotwood.

BETSEY. Why, bless my heart, you are a very baby! Why in the
name of heaven do you call this house 'The Rookery'?
There's not a rook near it!

MOTHER. The name was my dear husband's choice —

BETSEY. 'Cookery' would have been more to the purpose!
'The Rookery'! That was David Copperfield all over, that
was David Copperfield from head to foot! Calls a house a
rookery when there's not a bird to be seen! What do you call
your girl?

MOTHER. I don't know that it will be a girl, Miss Trotwood.

BETSEY. Bless the baby! I don't mean that. I mean your
servant girl.

MOTHER. Peggotty.

BETSEY. Peggotty? Do you mean to say, child, that any human being has gone into a Christian church, and got herself named Peggotty? Peggotty! Here, Peggotty! Your mistress is unwell. Fetch some tea and don't dawdle! You were talking about its being a girl? Never doubt that it will be a girl. I have a presentiment that it must be a girl. Now, when this girl is born –

MOTHER. Perhaps a boy –

MOTHER *goes into labour during next speech.*

BETSEY. Don't contradict! It is a girl! From the moment of this girl's birth, child, I intend to be her friend and her godmother, and I beg you'll call her Betsey Trotwood Copperfield. There must be no mistakes in life with *this* Betsey Trotwood. There must be no trifling with *her* affections. She must be well brought up, and well guarded. *She* will not repose foolish confidences where they are not deserved. I shall make that *my* care.

PEGGOTTY *comes in with the tea and then rushes to help* MOTHER *off.*

PEGGOTTY. Oh, my dear! Ma'am? Can you help me here?

BETSEY. Be quiet, girl! I'm talking to your mistress.

PEGGOTTY. Ma'am! You're a-talking to yourself! Oh, Lord, she's in a swoon! Send for the nurse! Upstairs with you, mistress! I'll boil up water! Ma'am! Send for the doctor!

General chaos: the bed is brought forward and MOTHER *pushed onto it as the* COMPANY *spin it round and circle with bowls of steaming water and towels.* DOCTOR *arrives with bag.* BETSEY *marches back and forth, barking: 'It must be a girl! It shall be a girl!' The* DOCTOR *delivers the baby, the bed disappears and* PEGGOTTY *and the* DOCTOR *come to* BETSEY, *beaming.*

Oh, ma'am! It's all over! The babe is born! Congratulations!

BETSEY. How is she?

DOCTOR. As comfortable as a young mother can be.

BETSEY. And *she*? How is *she*?

DOCTOR. 'She'?

BETSEY. The *baby*! How is *she*?

PEGGOTTY. She? She isn't a she. *She's* a boy. It's a *boy*!

> BETSEY *hits* PEGGOTTY *over the head with her bonnet and walks towards the* DOCTOR.

BETSEY. A boy? What nonsense! What absolute nonsense! What sort of doctor are you?

> *She chases the* DOCTOR *offstage.*

PEGGOTTY. Aunt Betsey Trotwood was gone, all the way back to Dover. You lay in your basket. Your mother lay in her bed. And we never saw, nor heard from Betsey again.

HAM. What? All because Master Davy is a boy?

DANIEL. What contrary daftness! What do you say, Em'ly? I bet you're well content he ain't a girl!

PEGGOTTY. As Davy is content, Em'ly is. What a fine little couple they makes.

DANIEL. Beautiful, they are together.

PEGGOTTY. The perfectest little couple, that play and sing all day, out on the beach picking shells and pebbles. Little Emily will break her heart unless you promise to come back, and to write to her until you do. Yarmouth and the sea will fade from our sight, and the salt tang of the air be lost in the dust of the country.

> *During the speech, the boat-house is taken off.*

Scene Four

YOUNG DAVID. We're home, Peggotty, we're home! Look, look! Where's Mother, Peggotty? Why hasn't she come to meet us?

PEGGOTTY. Master Davy, my love, I have to tell you something.

YOUNG DAVID. What's happened? Where's my mother? Peggotty! She's not dead, is she?

PEGGOTTY. No, of course not! It's not something bad, Davy, it's something good! What do you think, Davy? You've got a new father!

YOUNG DAVID. A father?

PEGGOTTY. A new one. Mr Murdstone.

YOUNG DAVID. Mr Murdstone? My new father...? Peggotty, I don't want a new father.

MOTHER *and* EDWARD MURDSTONE *are pushed on, sitting upright in the bed together.*

MOTHER. Davy!

MURDSTONE. Control yourself, Clara, my dear. Always control yourself. David? Come here, boy. How do you do, David?

YOUNG DAVID. How do you do, Mr Murdstone, sir?

MURDSTONE. Well, David. But you must not call me 'Mr Murdstone' any more. Now you must call me 'Father'.

YOUNG DAVID. Sir...? Father?

MURDSTONE. Good. You may kiss your mother.

YOUNG DAVID *and* MOTHER *kiss briefly, interrupted by* MURDSTONE.

Clara? Control. Firmness.

YOUNG DAVID *begins to cry.*

MOTHER. Oh, David, my child.

MURDSTONE. Now, is this firmness? David – come here.
(*Quietly, to* YOUNG DAVID *only.*) David, if I have a horse
or a dog to deal with, and it is obstinate, do you know what I
do? I beat him. I make him wince. I make him smart. I say to
myself, 'I'll conquer that fellow'; and if it cost him all the
blood he has, I do it. No son of mine will show weakness.
Now, tell me, what is that upon your face?

YOUNG DAVID. I think it must be dirt, sir.

MURDSTONE. You have a good deal of intelligence for a little
fellow. Take this handkerchief. Wipe your face. (*He
addresses* MOTHER.) Clara, my dear, you will not be
distressed any more, I hope. We shall soon improve our
youthful humours.

JANE MURDSTONE *sits bolt upright, from concealment in
the bed.*

JANE. Is that your boy, sister-in-law?

MOTHER. Davy, this is Mr Murdstone's sister, your new Aunt
Jane.

JANE. Generally speaking, I don't like boys. How do you do,
boy?

YOUNG DAVID. Very well, ma'am. I hope you are well.

JANE. He wants manners. Now, Clara, I am come here to
relieve you of all the trouble I can. You're much too pretty
and thoughtless to have any duties imposed upon you that
can be undertaken by me. If you'll be good enough to give
me your keys, I'll manage the household in future.

MOTHER. There is hardly need for that. I managed well
enough before I was married. I think I can continue to
manage now. I know my own house, after all.

JANE. *Your* house? I see.

MOTHER. Of course, now it is *our* house –

JANE. Let there be an end to this. I go tomorrow. Edward?

MOTHER. I am sure I don't want you to go –

MURDSTONE. Clara, you astound me. I knew I married a person inexperienced and artless, and hoped to form the person's character, and infuse into it some amount of firmness and decision. But when my sister is kind enough to come to my assistance, to assume, for my sake, a condition something like a housekeeper's, and meets from that person a base ingratitude –

MOTHER. Oh, Edward!

MURDSTONE. Base ingratitude, I say – my feelings may be chilled and altered.

MOTHER. Edward! Don't say that! Pray let us be friends. I couldn't live with coldness and unkindness. I am sorry. I know I have many defects, and it is very good of you to try to correct them for me. I can hardly object to Jane's desire to help me also.

MURDSTONE. Let there be no more harsh words. Give her your keys, Clara. Jane, this has not been your fault. You were betrayed into it by another.

MOTHER. Edward!

MURDSTONE. Clara! (*He registers* YOUNG DAVID*'s distress. He speaks gently, with apparent concern.*) This is not a fit scene for a little boy to witness. David? (*Beckoning* YOUNG DAVID *over to him.*) Go to your room. (*Checking* MOTHER*'s impulse.*) Clara!

YOUNG DAVID *goes to his 'room' – a luggage chest. He sits.*

CLOSE IN
ON CLARA

Scene Five

PEGGOTTY *makes the bed and moves it to a new position.*

PEGGOTTY (*to* YOUNG DAVID). After this night, Mrs
    Copperfield will never give opinion on any matter without
    first appealing to her sister-in-law, or first finding out what
    her sister-in-law's opinion is. And her sister-in-law will
    always have an opinion, and a harsh unbending one at that.
    She began her 'kind assistance' as soon as she was in the
    house. It consists mainly of moving everything in the
    storerooms to a different place, making havoc of any old
    arrangement with the local tradesfolk, and getting up before
    anyone else in the morning, to plunge into the servants'
    bedrooms on the suspicion –

JANE *dashes over and inspects under the bed, dashes back.*

– on the fixation – that they have a man concealed on the
    premises. Aggravating, but more daft than serious. Serious is
    when she turns her eye on Davy. *GL ARE AT
    PEGGOTY*

JANE. The boy.

MURDSTONE. The boy, Jane?

JANE. The boy should be sent away. To a school.

MOTHER. A school? But Davy learns well enough, here at
    home.

JANE. The boy should be sent away.

MURDSTONE. Jane! Enough. I shall be the judge. So, Clara,
    your son does well enough at home?

MOTHER. Why, yes, yes indeed, my dear.

MURDSTONE. Then let us see, shall we? David! Come here!
    Bring your Latin Grammar.

YOUNG DAVID. Yes, sir?

MURDSTONE. Is this his present lesson? There. Translate.

YOUNG DAVID *reads in Latin, stumbling more and more.*

JANE. He does not know it.

MOTHER. Oh, Davy, Davy!

MURDSTONE. Don't say 'Oh, Davy, Davy.' That's childish. Be firm with the boy. Either he knows his lesson or he does not know his lesson.

JANE. He does not know it.

MOTHER. Perhaps not all –

MURDSTONE. Then let us make him. Go to your room, sir, and learn this.

YOUNG DAVID *goes to his 'room'.*

Now, Clara. His lesson shall be learned. He shall be shut in his room until it is. And you must not visit him, or permit him to visit you.

JANE. Have no fear, Clara. We shall instruct him. Doubtless he is too much used to play. Children are by nature vicious.

PEGGOTTY. Vicious! I recall a child once was set among the Lord's Disciples!

MURDSTONE. You forget your place! It is the kitchen!

Scene Six

YOUNG DAVID *sits on the chest, swinging his legs until they come into contact with it.*

PEGGOTTY. So Davy will be locked in his room by the Murdstones for 'instruction', and the endless stone dullness of confinement might stupefy his mind, but for the providence of his dead father's books, ignored – under the bed – by his tormentors. These books are not the granite 'add, subtract, translate, divide' – they are *Robinson Crusoe*,

Don Quixote, *The Arabian Nights*, *Roderick Random* and
Peregrine Pickle, a glorious host which keeps him company
and keeps alive his fancy, if they can't in the end keep him
from the grinding Murdstones.

The actor who later plays DAVID *reads to his younger self.*

DAVID. 'The Grand Vizier had a daughter, Scheherazade, a
lady of courage, wit, and penetration, with so prodigious a
memory, that she never forgot anything, and her verse
exceeded the best poets of the time. Now it was the cruel
custom of the Sultan of those days, to wed a new wife every
night, and in the morning to have her strangled. But
Scheherazade had a design to stop the course of this
barbarity...'

MURDSTONE (*he has a cane, which he flexes*). I was flogged
myself, Clara. It did me no harm. As you can see.

MOTHER. Yes, dear, but –

MURDSTONE. Now, David, let us see what you have learned
today.   *UNFREEZE*

YOUNG DAVID *stumbles with the Latin again.*

JANE. He does not know it!

MOTHER. Oh, Davy! Edward, please –

MURDSTONE. We can hardly expect Clara to bear with
firmness the worry and torment which David has occasioned
her. Take her outside, Jane.

JANE *takes* MOTHER *a short distance away.*   *MOVE*
DOWNSTAGE RIGHT
David? Come here.

YOUNG DAVID. Please, Mr Murdstone, sir, don't beat me –

MURDSTONE. Come here!

YOUNG DAVID. I have tried to learn, honestly!

MURDSTONE. Come here!

He grabs YOUNG DAVID *and tries to beat him. They struggle, and* YOUNG DAVID *bites him.*

Aaaah! You vicious little brute!

MURDSTONE *begins to flog him. Freeze. The image of home disappears. The bed is now reduced to its boards to become the desks and benches of Salem House School, with* CREAKLE, TRADDLES *and* BOYS.

Scene Seven

CREAKLE. Put this round your neck.

He hands YOUNG DAVID *a placard on a string. It reads 'Take Care! He Bites!'*

TRADDLES. 'Take care! He bites!'

YOUNG DAVID. If you please, Mr Creakle, sir, isn't this for a dog?

CREAKLE. No, Copperfield. It ain't for a dog. It's for you. Mr Murdstone's firm instruction.

BOY (*pointing*). Watch out! He bites! Throw him a stick!

CREAKLE. Now, I know Mr Murdstone, and a worthy man he is. A man of firm, strong character, Mr Murdstone. He knows me, and I know him. And you will know me soon. Oh, yes, boy, you will know me soon. You will know that I'm impermeable. I say, and then I do. And when I say you'll do a thing, by gravel, I'll have it done! (*He goes, slicing the air with his cane.*)

TRADDLES. He wears a wig, you know.

YOUNG DAVID. What?

TRADDLES. Creakle. I'm Traddles. What's this for? You a dog or what?

BOY. Come on, boy, roll over!

TRADDLES. Have we to take you for walkies and call you
    Towzer?

BOY. Give us a paw!

Enter STEERFORTH, *a schoolboy. He is a young god.*

STEERFORTH. Stop that.

TRADDLES. Steerforth!

STEERFORTH. New boy, stop sniffing. What is your name?

YOUNG DAVID. Copperfield, sir.

STEERFORTH. Give me that placard.

YOUNG DAVID. If you please, sir, Mr Creakle said –

STEERFORTH. Never mind what he said. Give it here. (*He
    looks at it.*) This is a jolly shame. (*He tosses it aside.*)
    Copperfield shall sleep in my dorm. And I shall be his friend.
    Take his things up. I am pleased to meet you, Copperfield. I
    am Steerforth.

YOUNG DAVID. I am pleased to meet you, Steerforth.

STEERFORTH. Have you money with you, Copperfield? I will
    take care of it if you like. Though I won't, if you don't like.

YOUNG DAVID. Oh, please –

He hands a purse to STEERFORTH.

STEERFORTH. Do you want to spend anything now? You can
    if you like, you know. A couple of shillings on some almond
    cakes for the dormitory?

YOUNG DAVID. Oh, yes, of course.

STEERFORTH. And some currant wine as well? Just say the
    word.

YOUNG DAVID. Why, yes –

STEERFORTH. A shilling or so on biscuits, and another on fruit? I say, young Copperfield, you're going it! You really should try to make it stretch, you know! But look here, you've not to worry. About Creakle and the other boys and so forth. I'll take care of you, young 'un. As long as we're together, you can rely on Steerforth.

Scene Eight

TRADDLES. Creakle, our iron-hard headmaster, is a dunce.

YOUNG DAVID. His only skill is flogging boys, and roaring –

BOY. '*What I say, I do!*'

TRADDLES. Half the boys are beaten before the day's teaching's begun –

BOY. The other half before it has ended.

YOUNG DAVID. Only Steerforth is exempt. Creakle would not dare face that cool stare and matchless courage.

TRADDLES. Besides, Steerforth is his best scholar, and his best-connected scholar –

BOY. And Creakle is too near bankruptcy not to toady for all he is worth.

TRADDLES. Steerforth dines with him.

BOY. Steerforth walks to church with him.

TRADDLES. Steerforth dances with his daughter.

STEERFORTH. Copperfield?

YOUNG DAVID. Steerforth?

STEERFORTH *gives* YOUNG DAVID *his shoes to clean: the other* BOYS *are deeply jealous of this 'honour'.*

STEERFORTH. Your father is dead, I believe.

YOUNG DAVID. Yes, Steerforth.

STEERFORTH. So is my father. This must be what unites us, so: we are both pampered by our mothers... You haven't got a sister, have you?

YOUNG DAVID. No, Steerforth.

STEERFORTH. That's a pity. If you had one, I think she would have been a pretty, timid, little bright-eyed sort of a girl. I should have liked to know her. Ah, well.

YOUNG DAVID. Sorry, Steerforth.

CREAKLE. Silence! Open your books!

The SCHOOLBOYS *begin to murmur, in unison, a Latin passage. This continues under all of the following speech.*

Now, boys, take care what you're about. Come fresh up to the lessons, or I'll come fresh up to the punishment. I won't flinch, oh no. I won't flinch. Get yourselves good marks for your work, boys, or I shall give you marks, oh yes, I shall give you marks. You, Copperfield! Here! Now, Copperfield, you are said to be known for biting. Well, I am known for biting too. (*He shows* YOUNG DAVID *his cane, and punctuates his speech by threatening him with it.*) What do you think of that for a tooth! Is it a sharp tooth, hey? Is it a double tooth, hey? It is a wisdom tooth! A wisdom tooth! D'you feel it bite, hey? Do you feel it bite? But Copperfield! Where is your sign? Where is your sign, you insolent boy?

STEERFORTH. I took it off him. It was a jolly shame.

CREAKLE. What? You took it off him? Well... Well done, Mr Steerforth. Ha, well done, I say. The wretched thing would have got in the way of my cane. It would have got in the way of my wisdom. We wouldn't want Copperfield denied my wisdom, would we, hey? Would we, Traddles, you stupid, staring boy!

The Latin murmuring begins again, accompanied by a rhythmic arithmetic table. CREAKLE *exits, swishing his cane.*

Scene Nine

STEERFORTH. I think we've had enough of Creakle's wisdom
for one day.

TRADDLES. Only three months, one day and four hours left.

YOUNG DAVID. Then what?

TRADDLES. Christmas holidays.

STEERFORTH. I shall expire of boredom long before then. I
assume it is pointless to enquire if anyone can provide
intelligent entertainment fit for a gentleman?

BOY. I know a trick with a lighted taper –

STEERFORTH. Intelligent and fit for a gentleman, I said.

YOUNG DAVID. If you please, Steerforth…

STEERFORTH. Yes, Copperfield?

YOUNG DAVID. I have read some stories, with good heroes,
Ali Baba, *The Arabian Nights*, *Don Quixote* and such like.

STEERFORTH. Oh, yes?

YOUNG DAVID. Well, I think I could tell them over, if you
would like. They are very clear in my memory.

STEERFORTH. Do these heroes have much to do with Latin
Grammar?

YOUNG DAVID. No, none at all.

TRADDLES. Or get their ears boxed with Greek primers?

YOUNG DAVID. Never.

STEERFORTH. Then I appoint you our chief storyteller, young
Copperfield. You must keep our spirits up until the holidays
bring escape to the love and kindness of our families.

A pause in which the stage darkens around **YOUNG
DAVID**, *then –*

YOUNG DAVID. Well, um... there was this, um, man... called Sinbad, who lived in Arabia. Sinbad was a great sailor, and went on lots of voyages to strange lands where he had exciting adventures, and once upon a time he and his companions came upon a desert island where they saw a great huge big white egg the size of a church lying on the sand. Now, this was the egg of the biggest bird in the whole wide world, the giant roc. Before Sinbad could stop them, some of the sailors threw stones at the egg and broke it. And at once the island went dark and cold. A huge shadow blotted out the sun. The roc was coming. Sinbad and the others fled back to their ship, hauled up the anchor and set sail, but all too soon the giant roc came flying after them with what looked like half a mountain clasped in its massive talons. And when it was right above the ship, so that the sailors below could hardly see the sky, it dropped the mountain, and the poor little ship was swamped...

Scene Ten

The stage floods with light, and the BOYS *flee, hauling the bed off and singing a Christmas carol.* YOUNG DAVID *is left alone and apprehensive. Enter* PEGGOTTY.

PEGGOTTY. Master Davy!

YOUNG DAVID. Peggotty!

PEGGOTTY. Master Davy, my love. Welcome home! Let me look at you. My, how you've growed. Mistress Copperfield – he's home, Master Davy's home!

MOTHER. Davy, my dear, my own dear boy!

They embrace.

Oh, what a little man you are becoming! Oh, Davy, I have such a wonder to show you. Come here. This little tiny thing, Davy, is your baby brother. Is he not beautiful?

YOUNG DAVID. Oh, Mother! He is – perfect.

MOTHER *gives him the baby.*

Hello, little brother.

MOTHER. Ah, Davy, what a loving boy you are.

PEGGOTTY. And what a loving brother he will be.

YOUNG DAVID. Peggotty, I have a message from the carter who fetched me home. He says to tell you 'Barkis is willing – and waiting.'

PEGGOTTY. Drat the man. He wants to marry me. Did you ever hear such a proposal, mistress? 'Barkis is willing' indeed!

MOTHER. Why, Davy, Peggotty has made a catch! Barkis is willing and waiting!

Enter JANE. *UPSTAGE RIGHT*

JANE (*screaming*). The baby!

MOTHER. What is it?

JANE. The boy has got the baby! Edward! Edward!

Enter MURDSTONE.

MURDSTONE. What is this?

MOTHER. My dear –

JANE. Edward – the boy was holding your baby!

MURDSTONE. Clara? Is this true?

MOTHER. There is surely no harm –

MURDSTONE. Never touch my baby again. Do you hear? Never.

PEGGOTTY. But Mr Murdstone, his own brother –

MURDSTONE. Your place is the kitchen.

He points off. PEGGOTTY *goes.* MURDSTONE *turns to* YOUNG DAVID.

How long are you here for?

YOUNG DAVID. A month, sir. I beg your pardon, sir. I am very sorry. I did not mean –

JANE. A month? Starting when?

YOUNG DAVID. Today, Aunt.

JANE. Good. That's one day off then.

MURDSTONE. There is a stiff Latin task waiting in your room. I will bring you another tomorrow. You will keep to your room, sir, and not distress your mother. She is quite busy enough with our new child. And I forbid you absolutely to visit that creature in the kitchen.

YOUNG DAVID *retreats to his room, where he begins to read a book.* DAVID *appears.*

DAVID (*reading to* YOUNG DAVID). 'What have I done,' cried the miserable Aladdin, 'to be treated with such severity?' 'I have my reasons,' said his uncle, 'and I supply the place of your father.' And Aladdin grew afraid, and prayed that his uncle would help him from the darkness of the cave. 'Give me the lamp,' said his uncle. 'Give me first the lamp.'

Scene Eleven

School is re-established with bedframe and BOYS.

STEERFORTH. Well, young Copperfield, here we go again. I hope the Christmas jollities with your indulgent mother have not been entirely exhausting, and that you've kept up with your reading. I rely upon you for that, I really do.

YOUNG DAVID. Do you, Steerforth? I have, you know!

STEERFORTH. Well?

YOUNG DAVID. Well… on one of Sinbad's voyages he had to escape from a giant man!

STEERFORTH. How?

YOUNG DAVID. In a rowing boat!

STEERFORTH. Come on then!

They make a 'boat' – perhaps from the bed.

YOUNG DAVID. The giant man was as tall as a palm tree, with one eye in the middle of his forehead, as red as a burning coal, his teeth were long and sharp, his ears like an elephant, and his nails like the talons of a great bird –

CREAKLE (*off*). Silence! Open your books!

STEERFORTH. Did he wear a wig?

They fall about laughing and dismantle the 'boat'. Enter CREAKLE. *The* BOYS *begin to chant a Latin passage.*

CREAKLE. Now, boys, take care. Come fresh up to lessons, or I'll come fresh up to punishment. Get yourselves good marks, boys, or I shall give you marks. You, Traddles! What do you think of that, hey? It is a wisdom tooth! A wisdom tooth! D'you feel it bite, hey? Do you feel it bite? Traddles, you stupid, staring boy!

STEERFORTH. The wine of Mr Creakle's wisdom has not improved with age.

CREAKLE. Copperfield. Copperfield, come here to me… Stand up. I'm not going to beat you… I have something particular hard to impart, Copperfield.

YOUNG DAVID. Sir?

CREAKLE. A gritty lesson, I fear, Copperfield. But we all have to learn it. When you came away from home, was your mama well?

YOUNG DAVID. Yes, sir.

CREAKLE. I have to tell you – she is now very ill.

YOUNG DAVID. Sir?

CREAKLE. Very dangerously ill.

YOUNG DAVID. Mr Creakle?

CREAKLE. Copperfield… she is dead.

Scene Twelve

A funeral cortège is formed and MOTHER*'s body is buried in the well of the bedframe.*

YOUNG DAVID (*sings*).
    Abide with me, fast falls the eventide,
    The darkness deepens; Lord with me abide.
    When other helpers fail and comfort flee,
    Help of the helpless, O abide with me.
The bed is taken off.

JANE. I have given the Peggotty creature notice to quit. She has requested that the boy go with her to Yarmouth for two weeks.

MURDSTONE. He will be idle there. Idleness is the root of evil.

JANE. He will be idle here. Cannot he be returned to school?

    MURDSTONE *does not reply.*

    Are we to be plagued by his sullenness at home then?

MURDSTONE. I have suffered enough discomfort. Let her have him in Yarmouth. (*To* YOUNG DAVID.) Go pack your bags, sir. You are leaving.

Scene Thirteen

The bed returns as PEGGOTTY*'s boat-house.* PEGGOTTY *is singing a jolly song.*

DANIEL. Master Davy! Ham, Emily, see who's come here! Give me your hand, master. Right welcome you are aboard, and all the more so for your present trouble. We are a rough family, sir, but a true family: and a family ready enough for you, if you drop anchor with us.

YOUNG DAVID. Oh, Mr Peggotty, I am ready for your family!

DANIEL. Well said, Master Davy. You and me, Ham and Little Emily, all together!

PEGGOTTY. What a pass we have come to, that a young gentleman like our Davy should need us for his family.

DANIEL. What about that great aunt of his?

PEGGOTTY. Betsey Trotwood? What good to him is she? She's sulked in Dover ever since he had the audacity to be born a boy.

YOUNG DAVID. Where is Little Emily?

DANIEL. Ha! She's a-hiding, she is. (*To* PEGGOTTY.) A little puss, it is!

YOUNG DAVID. Hiding? Hiding from me, you mean? Why?

PEGGOTTY. A little puss, indeed. Well, brother Daniel, if we are to be family for Master Davy, you'd best know it's a family as is growing.

EMILY *comes in, balancing a book on her head.*

You are looking at an affianced woman. 'Barkis the Willing' has waited enough. Barkis and me is to be married.

DANIEL. My life, Clara – marriage, is it? (*Drawing* YOUNG DAVID*'s attention to* EMILY.) Davy?

EMILY. Oh, it's you, is it?

YOUNG DAVID. Emily...

He tries to kiss her, but she makes him kiss her hand while she curtsies in an exaggeratedly ladylike manner. She laughs at his confusion.

EMILY. Oh, Davy: you are a silly boy!

EMILY *and* YOUNG DAVID *move away.*

PEGGOTTY. Davy's little sweetheart is growing up.

DANIEL. Aye, she likes to play the little woman.

PEGGOTTY. He'll love her all the more for it.

DANIEL. Come back and wed her, eh?

PEGGOTTY. She could do worse, Dan. Much worse.

Scene Fourteen

YOUNG DAVID. Will you write to me when I'm at school again, Em?

EMILY. Go on, Davy! What would I write about?

YOUNG DAVID. Well – what you'd been doing, what Mr Peggotty was about – and Ham.

EMILY. I'll have been to school and done needlework, Uncle Dan will have been sorting crabs and crawfish, and Ham repairing boats. You know all that. And I've told it you. Now. Why would you want me to write it?

YOUNG DAVID. When I'm at school, Em, I'll want reminding.

EMILY. You mean you'll forget all about me if I don't write.

YOUNG DAVID. No. But if you write, I'll see the sky here and smell the sea. And I'll see the boat-house and the family and I'll see you, Emily.

EMILY. You must make friends at school, Davy.

YOUNG DAVID. I have a friend. And a really special one, too.
Steerforth – the best boy in the school. He's astonishingly
clever. He knows everything. He is the best cricketer you
ever saw. He will give you as many men as you like at
draughts and still win easily. He sings and he plays and he's
handsome, he's noble, he's generous and he's brave. He is
my friend, Emily, and he's the most perfect gentleman you
could ever wish to see.

EMILY. Then I should wish to see him, Davy. If he is your
friend. I will write to you about here, and you must write to
me about there. I will tell you about Uncle Dan and Ham,
and you will tell me about Steerforth and your school.

The scene is dismissed by MURDSTONE.

MURDSTONE. School? You will not return to school.
Education is costly. To the young this is a world for action.
Do you know what a counting-house is? No? Then it is time
to learn. I have secured your employment in one. Murdstone
and Grinby's. It is in London. So – you are provided for. Do
not unpack your bags.

Scene Fifteen

Murdstone and Grinby's warehouse, busy with WORKERS
*singing 'Ten Green Bottles'. The bed is transformed with crates
and bottles, a factory line is set up.*

MICK. You the new boy?

YOUNG DAVID. David Copperfield.

MEALY. Thought you was Murdstone.

YOUNG DAVID. No, Copperfield. What do we do here?

MAN. Bottles.

GIRL. We clean bottles.

YOUNG DAVID. Is that all?

MEALY. Cork bottles.

MICK. Seal bottles.

MAN. Crate bottles.

MICK. There's a lot of variety.

MEALY. With bottles.

YOUNG DAVID. What is to be learned here, is learned in minutes. After that: bottles. Nothing more is taught me. I have no books. I have no friends, and no one cares for me. I am alone. My life is being bottled up. When the cork is quite pushed home, I'll be with them in the song.

MICK. Oi! Coppertop! There's a man for you.

Enter MICAWBER.

YOUNG DAVID. Oh, thank you. Mr...?

MICAWBER. Micawber, my dear sir, Micawber. I have received a letter from the excellent Mr Grinby which desires me to receive you as a paying guest into an apartment within my domestic habitation. This residence is to be found at Windsor Terrace, on the City Road of this great capital. In short – I live there, and you are to lodge there. Under the impression that your peregrinations in this metropolis have not as yet been extensive, and that you might have some difficulty in penetrating the arcana of the modern Babylon – in short, you might get lost – I shall call again this evening and install in you the knowledge of the nearest way. I beg to wish you good day, Master Copperfield, sir. I will intrude no longer.

MEALY. Well, cork me in a bottle. What was that all about?

MICK. Cop's got new lodgings. I think.

They resume singing, and haul the bed to a new position for the next scene: the MICAWBERS.

Scene Sixteen

MRS MICAWBER. I never thought, when I lived with Mama and Papa, that I should ever find it necessary to take a lodger. But Mr Micawber being in difficulties, all considerations of private feeling must give way.

YOUNG DAVID. Yes, ma'am.

MRS MICAWBER. Mr Micawber's difficulties are almost overwhelming just at present, but know, Mr Copperfield – I shall never desert him.

YOUNG DAVID. Yes indeed, ma'am.

MRS MICAWBER. If Mr Micawber's creditors will not give him time, why, they must take the consequences, and the sooner they bring it to an issue the better. Blood cannot be obtained from a stone. Neither can anything – at present – be obtained from Mr Micawber. But I must not trouble you with our concerns, Mr Copperfield, though I know I can rely on your discretion.

YOUNG DAVID. Oh, yes, ma'am. Yes indeed.

CREDITORS (*off, shouting*). Pay us, will you? You can't hide! Pay us! Swindlers! Robbers! Pay us!

MICAWBER makes a spectacular, melodramatic entrance, razor in hand.

MICAWBER. I can stand this mortification no longer! I am a gentleman after all, with gentle sensibilities! My love! One last look upon your lovely face, then –

MRS MICAWBER. Micawber! No!

MICAWBER. There is no other way, my love!

He sees YOUNG DAVID. His manner changes abruptly. He is calm and conversational.

Oh, hullo, Copperfield. Settling in?

YOUNG DAVID. Eh, yes, thank you, Mr Micawber.

MICAWBER. Perhaps you would do me the honour of taking a veal cutlet at our table this evening?

CREDITORS (*off, shouting*). Pay us, will you? You can't hide! Pay us! Swindlers! Robbers! Pay us!

MICAWBER. I shall throw myself from Blackfriars Bridge!

MRS MICAWBER. Micawber!

YOUNG DAVID. This is *Don Quixote*!

MICAWBER. I shall polish my shoes and eat a lamb chop.

YOUNG DAVID. Or *Sinbad the Sailor*!

MRS MICAWBER. The silver spoons Mama presented me.

MICAWBER. Some warm ale, Mr Copperfield?

MRS MICAWBER. Perhaps you would carry them to the pawnbroker?

The CREDITORS *break in and manhandle* MICAWBER.

MICAWBER. Gentlemen, wait! (*To* YOUNG DAVID.) Um, you couldn't let me have a shilling, to tip the porter? Even now there are some appearances best kept up! See, I have written a bill for the said shilling, for you to place with Mrs Micawber, on most strict terms to honour my oath and restore that shilling to you, upon – the first opportunity. Farewell, Mr Copperfield, farewell!

MICAWBER *is taken by the* CREDITORS *and deposited in the bed, staring out through the bars.*

YOUNG DAVID. Ali Baba!

MRS MICAWBER. Oh, dear Mr Copperfield, catastrophe!

YOUNG DAVID. Whatever is the matter, Mrs Micawber?

MRS MICAWBER. Mr Micawber is arrested and carried to the King's Bench Prison! We have fallen. Fallen, never to rise again!

MICAWBER. My love!

MRS MICAWBER. My love. I will never desert you.

MICAWBER. Take warning by my fate, I conjure you, young friend! If a man has twenty pound a year, and spends nineteen pounds nineteen and sixpence, he is happy; but if he spends twenty-one, he is miserable.

MRS MICAWBER. Perhaps Mr Copperfield would join us for supper on Saturday?

MICAWBER. Say 'yes', Mr Copperfield, say 'yes'! We will not take 'no' for an answer! My dear, what a splendid idea!

MRS MICAWBER. I will never desert you!

MICAWBER. My love!

MRS MICAWBER. My love!

MICAWBER. An evening promenade, my friend?

MRS MICAWBER. A game of casino, Mr Copperfield?

YOUNG DAVID. The Micawbers... The Micawbers, my new *Arabian Nights*!

MICAWBER *steps free from the 'prison'*.

MICAWBER. I am emancipated, Mr Copperfield, unfettered, and my autonomy restored under the Insolvent Debtors Act of the Houses of Parliament – in short, I am free.

MRS MICAWBER. We are to go to Plymouth, Mr Copperfield. My family hope to find a place there for Mr Micawber, in the customs house. Mr Micawber shall flourish in that interesting business, for he is a man of indisputable talent.

MICAWBER. And if a place *does* turn up, I shall be ready!

MRS MICAWBER (*dissolving in tears*). Oh, Micawber!

MICAWBER. My love?

MRS MICAWBER. I shall never desert you! Do not for one moment think it! I never will do that!

MICAWBER. Rest assured, my love, I never thought you would.

MRS MICAWBER. No, no! Don't ask me! I never will! Mr
Micawber has his faults, Mr Copperfield: he has been –
improvident! But I never will desert him!

MICAWBER. Copperfield, farewell! Every happiness and
prosperity! Let my blighted destiny be a warning to you!
And if anything turns up, of which I am actually rather
confident, I shall be happy if it is in my power to improve
your prospects! And now, *adieu, mon brave, adieu!*

MEALY. Cork me in a bottle, what was that about?

MICK. I dunno. But I tell you what: Coppertop needs new
lodgings.

They sing 'Ten Green Bottles'.

YOUNG DAVID. No. I don't want lodgings. I want to run
away. I can't go home. I can't go to Peggotty – Murdstone
will look for me there straight off. And Yarmouth, would be
pretty soon after. And I have no one else, except that Great
Aunt Betsey, Peggotty told me of. I'll run to Aunt Betsey, in
Dover. Like Sinbad, I'll find safe harbour if I never give up
hope.

The bed is removed. YOUNG DAVID *journeys to Dover. He
is steadily deprived of bag, money, coat, shoes, and food by a
series of terrifying caricatures of* PETTY THIEVES,
TRAMPS *and* CONSTABLES, *until he is ragged, exhausted
and filthy. The actor who later plays* DAVID *haunts him.*

Please, sir, can I have a ride?

DAVID. Sinbad! Sinbad! Beware the old man of the sea!

MAN. Where did you get that shilling, you varmint? (*Snatches
it.*) I'll fetch the police! Police! Police! (*He exits.*)

YOUNG DAVID *offers his waistcoat to a* PAWNBROKER.

YOUNG DAVID. I need some money!

PAWNBROKER. Let's have that waistcoat, then.

DAVID. A giant bird, with wings so huge they blot out the sun.

PAWNBROKER (*snatching waistcoat*). Get out of my shop, you thieving ragamuffin.

YOUNG DAVID. My money! My money!

DAVID. The ship is sinking. Sinbad – the ship is sinking!

YOUNG DAVID. The waves are like mountains.

A THIEF *steals his bag.*

DAVID. What good are all your diamonds now?

YOUNG DAVID. Alms for the poor, in Allah's name!

MAN. What's this? Begging, are you? You're nothing but a thief, damn you!

WOMAN. What game are you on?

DAVID. They are cannibals! Flee for your life – they are cannibals!

MAN. Let's have a look at those boots!

WOMAN. That's my brother's hat! Give it here!

They steal YOUNG DAVID*'s hat and boots.*

DAVID. You are alone, Sinbad. The ship has sailed without you. You are alone on this desert isle.

YOUNG DAVID*'s assailants mock him with donkey-like braying, flapping their hands beside their ears, until* BETSEY TROTWOOD *storms on.*

Scene Seventeen

BETSEY. How many times have I told you boys to KEEP THOSE DONKEYS OFF MY LAWN!

The assailants flee.

YOUNG DAVID. If you please, Mrs Trotwood...

BETSEY. NO DONKEYS AND NO BOYS! ... NO BOYS!

YOUNG DAVID. Aunt Betsey? If you please, I am your nephew.

BETSEY. What? My nephew?

YOUNG DAVID. David Copperfield. You were there when I was born, and saw my dear mama. She is dead now. And I have been very unhappy. I was taken from school and sent to work as a warehouse boy, but I have run away. I've been walking for six days. All my things have been stolen and I've been sleeping in haystacks –

BETSEY. Run away?

YOUNG DAVID. Run away to you, Aunt Betsey. Please don't send me back. Please, Aunt Betsey.

BETSEY. Mr Dick! I wish to speak to you.

DICK *comes on, carrying the tail of a kite.*

DICK. Miss Trotwood?

BETSEY. Mr Dick. You are not to be a fool, now.

DICK. Yes. No.

BETSEY. Mr Dick. You have heard me mention David Copperfield.

DICK. David Copperfield?

BETSEY. This is his son. He has run away. If he had been born a girl, he would not have run away, but he has.

DICK. No.Yes.

BETSEY. So, Mr Dick, here is young David Copperfield. David, this is Mr Dick, a good and trusted friend. I put it to you, Mr Dick – and I want some sound advice, some very sound advice – young David Copperfield: what shall we do with him?

DICK. Yes. No. I see. I think... I should wash him!

BETSEY. Mr Dick – you set us all right. Heat the bath!

The bed is brought on as a bath. YOUNG DAVID *is helped in as 'hot water' is poured over him and his back well and truly scrubbed.* YOUNG DAVID *is bathed and toweled, during which –*

Whatever possessed that poor unfortunate baby, his mother, that she must go and be married again!

DICK. Perhaps she fell in love.

BETSEY. Fell in love! What – to fix her simple faith on a perfect dog of a man, certain to ill use her? She had had one husband. She had given birth to this child standing here – what more could she want? And where was this child's sister Betsey? Not forthcoming! Not forthcoming! And she marries again – marries this murderer, or some such name! And then that woman with the pagan name, that Peggotty – she goes and gets married! Has she not seen enough of the evil attending such things? Now, Mr Dick! I am going to ask you another question. Look at this child, David Copperfield's son. What would you do with him now?

DICK. Oh! Yes. Ah. I think... I think – I should put him – to bed.

BETSEY. Yes! Mr Dick – you set us all right, again. We'll put this child to bed!

The COMPANY *make up the bed, fluffing up the pillows and cocooning* YOUNG DAVID *in a sea of white linen. Finally a coverlet flutters down and the picture is complete.*

Boy – young David Copperfield, so like your poor baby of a mama – your flinty old Aunt Betsey Trotwood has decided that she can't have her nephew prowling and wandering. She is going to take you in, and defy these Murdstones. I shall adopt you, and set my lawyer Wickfield in Canterbury to find you a school.

DICK. Hurrah!

BETSEY. Mr Dick? You are not to be a fool! To make up for not being a girl, this boy must be called David *Trotwood* Copperfield. Well, what do you say?

DICK. Who? Me? Oh... A new name goes with a new life.

DAVID. Sinbad – you are home!

Scene Eighteen

YOUNG DAVID *in bed. Enter* DICK *with a huge kite.*

YOUNG DAVID (*half-asleep*). A gigantic bird with wings so huge it blocked out the sun.

DICK. What do you think of this for a kite?

YOUNG DAVID. I think it's beautiful, Mr Dick.

DICK. I made it. Some people think I'm a fool, you know. But not your aunt. We'll go and fly it, you and I.

YOUNG DAVID. Why is there writing on it?

DICK. Those are the facts about King Charles the First and his troubles, and how all those facts are in *my* head now that *his* head is cut off, and I fly the kite ever so high, and the King Charles's facts are blown away by the wind and so forth. It's my manner of diffusing 'em. I don't know where they come down, but I take my chance with that.

YOUNG DAVID. I see.

DICK. But it's worth taking a chance, 'cos it's lots of fun! Come on!

He skips about with YOUNG DAVID. *Enter* DAVID, *who takes over the kite.* YOUNG DAVID *exits.*

BETSEY. David Trotwood Copperfield, you must receive an education befitting a gentleman. I have seen my lawyer Wickfield in Canterbury, and we have secured you a place there, in the school of the excellent Dr Strong. Well, Mr Dick? We shall make our young David a proper gentleman. What do you think of that?

DICK. A proper gentleman? David, a proper gentleman? Well, then – I think I should dress him.

BETSEY. Mr Dick, you have the right of it, again. We cannot send this boy into society in rags and cast-offs. A waistcoat – nothing too fanciful or frenchified, but he must have a waistcoat. Indifferent I may be to public opinion and the vagaries of fashion, but no proper gentleman is without a waistcoat. Now, David, though your new school is in Canterbury, you are not to be afraid that I am sending you away. This is now, and always will be, your home. And I have no intention that David Trotwood Copperfield should board with strangers in a strange town. Not after the life he has endured. No. David shall lodge with Mr Wickfield and his daughter, Agnes, as one of his family. It's a capital house for study, quiet and roomy and prettily furnished, with a piano and a whole library of books. Wickfield is a quiet, retiring, gentle soul. And then there's his daughter, Agnes.

AGNES WICKFIELD *enters.*

Little Agnes Wickfield has been her father's housekeeper since her poor mother passed away. You two young creatures have much in common – why, David, you are so alike, she might be your very sister. I am sure she will welcome a companion of her own age.

Scene Nineteen

AGNES *teases* DAVID *with his school report.*

AGNES (*reading*). 'Geography: could do better'!

DAVID. Oh, Agnes! Dr Strong's school is excellent, so different from my last school, where the master beat us every day. Dr Strong beats no one; instead he appeals in all things to the honour and good faith of us boys. And we do our best to do him credit.

AGNES (*reading*). 'Mathematics: very good. Latin – '

AGNES *runs off.* DAVID *explores and finds a large trunk. He peeps in, is startled by what he sees and snaps it shut. It opens – and* URIAH HEEP *climbs out.*

URIAH. Good evening, Master Copperfield. Mr Wickfield told me to expect you. My name is Heep. Uriah Heep.

DAVID. How – how do you do, Uriah?

URIAH. So how do you find the school, Master Copperfield? Your old Dr Strong sounds an excellent man, Master Copperfield. And Mr Wickfield is a most excellent man.

DAVID. Of that I am certain, Uriah. For he has taken me into his home, to oblige my aunt.

URIAH. Your aunt is a sweet lady, Master Copperfield. A sweet lady. I suppose you stop here some time, Master Copperfield?

DAVID. I believe I am to be brought up here, as long as I remain at Dr Strong's school.

URIAH. I should think that then you will come into the business, Master Copperfield.

DAVID. What, Mr Wickfield's business? I think not, Uriah. No such scheme is entertained in my behalf by anybody.

URIAH. Oh, Master Copperfield, I should think you would!

Enter AGNES.

Miss Agnes, good evening to you!

AGNES. Still here, Uriah? You were surely finished your
accounting an age ago. We must not keep Master David from
his studies, you know.

URIAH. Oh, Miss Agnes! Master Copperfield! I hope I know
my 'umble place! I would not dream –

AGNES. I have set a little supper in the kitchen. I am sure there
is enough for three. I know you are humble, Uriah, but I
think you may be hungry, too.

Exit URIAH.

If I'm to be your sister, David Trotwood Copperfield, you
have to tell me everything that happens to you at Dr Strong's
and all about your other family of friends in Yarmouth, and
your childhood sweetheart Emily, and the admirable
Steerforth.

PEGGOTTY (*entering to tidy bed away*). At last Davy has
found his family, and a proper schooling with the good Dr
Strong. And Davy has growed into a man, and a powerful
strong scholar. For in the end my Davy was Dr Strong's head
boy, and a very Steerforth to the other boys. Agnes Wickfield
is a true heart, and she'll keep a proper eye on our Davy, of
that I have no doubt. So all is well with our boy, and I can
turn to my new task, for 'willin'' Barkis is become a 'doin''
Barkis. I am a married woman now – Clara Peggotty Barkis,
if you please – and my first care must be my new husband,
Lord love him. And if he's now for 'doin'', he'll find me
more than willing.

PEGGOTTY *exits*.

AGNES. Tell me about Miss Shepherd, your partner at the
dancing school.

DAVID. Oh, how I loved her! Her round face and her flaxen hair
– once I kissed her in the cloakroom! Oh, bliss unblemished –

AGNES. Until you met Miss Larkins, and discovered silk cravats.

DAVID. Miss Larkins was a reputed beauty.

AGNES. Miss Larkins was twenty-eight.

DAVID. Agnes, you are cruel.

AGNES. David, I am honest.

DAVID. Oh, Agnes! What should I do without you? Who should I turn to for advice?

URIAH. Mistress Agnes, Master Copperfield. Forgive my unseemly intrusion, but it's Mr Wickfield.

AGNES. Father!

URIAH. He is a little, ah, distressed.

AGNES. No, David, stay here. He would not wish you to see him like this.

AGNES *goes*.

URIAH. The sad memory of his late wife was brought to his mind, he has refreshed himself with some claret, and is confused somewhat, and tearful. I have been trying to help him to his room.

DAVID. You are working late tonight, Uriah.

URIAH. I am improving my legal knowledge, Master Copperfield. I have been going through Tidd's *Practice*. Oh, what a writer Mr Tidd is, Master Copperfield.

DAVID. You must hope to become a great lawyer, to bury yourself in such dry study.

URIAH. Me, Master Copperfield? Oh, no! I'm a very 'umble person. The 'umblest person going, let the other be who he may. How much have I to be thankful for, in working for Mr Wickfield.

DAVID. Indeed, Uriah. Mr Wickfield is most generous.

URIAH. I know it, and I am thankful for it, Master Copperfield. This very night, in his generosity, he has promised to make me his clerk, that I might indeed become a lawyer – of a very 'umble sort – which would otherwise not lie within my lowly means.

DAVID. Perhaps one day Mr Wickfield's generosity may make you a partner in his business, Uriah.

URIAH. Oh, Master Copperfield, no! I am much too 'umble for that. Besides, how could I compete with such a rival as yourself?

DAVID. I am not your rival!

URIAH. No, Master Copperfield? Will not Mr Wickfield make you his partner, when you and Miss Agnes are married?

DAVID. What? Miss Wickfield is very dear to me, Uriah, as a sister. But only as a sister, I assure you. And I don't intend to marry her for a partnership.

URIAH. Yet everyone must have an admiration for Miss Agnes.

DAVID. Why, yes – yes indeed.

URIAH. Everyone. However 'umble.

AGNES *returns, concealing her anxiety for her father.*

Miss Agnes. Mr Wickfield is... settled?

AGNES. Yes, thank you. Goodnight, Uriah.

URIAH. Goodnight, miss. Master Copperfield.

He goes.

DAVID. Agnes?

AGNES. My father has retired for the night. Memories of Mama always affect him cruelly. The wine bottle offers him a little solace, but never enough, I fear. Where were we?

DAVID. I was undertaking always to turn to you for advice – I am concerned for Mr Wickfield.

AGNES. Do not be. He works too hard, that is all. Do you think my advice so sound, that you will always seek it?

DAVID. You are always right, and yet in checking my follies you always make me laugh. I shall never cease to love you.

AGNES. You talk as if I were the late Miss Larkins.

DAVID. Abuse my confidences if you will, but I'll go on confiding in you just the same. You cannot stop me. Whenever I fall into trouble, or fall in love, I shall always tell you – even when I come to fall in love in earnest.

AGNES. But you have always been in earnest!

DAVID. Oh, stop! Times have changed since I was a green schoolboy. Know, oh mocking one, that I, David Copperfield, am invited, as an articled clerk, in the firm of Spenlow and Jorkins, by no lesser a personage than Mr Spenlow himself –

AGNES. Yes?

DAVID. To provide an escort to his dismal daughter Dora, to an even more dismal ball when she comes home from her dismal finishing school in Paris.

AGNES. Is she so awful, then?

DAVID. She's Spenlow's daughter, Agnes.

AGNES. Now it's you who are cruel. Condemning a poor girl you have never met. It would serve you right if she was beautiful and charming and spurned you completely.

DAVID. Beautiful and charming? Have you seen old Spenlow?

Enter DORA, *as if for the ball, a vision of doll-like loveliness.* DAVID *is instantly smitten.*

My God, Agnes! Have you ever seen such curls? I – love her!

AGNES *discreetly withdraws.*

DORA. Mr Copperfield.

DAVID (*stammering*). Sh-shall we walk, Miss Spenlow?

DORA. My father is quite absurd, Mr Copperfield. Do you
know he dislikes me walking in the garden in the morning,
because it is too early for the day to have been properly
aired? I tell him I must come out, it's the brightest time to
walk, it's the only time to walk! Don't you think so?

DAVID. W-why, Miss Spenlow – it – it is very – bright to me
this evening, though before I saw you it seemed quite – dark.

DORA. Do you mean a compliment, or that the weather's
changed?

DAVID. The weather? No – but – It was no compliment, Miss
Spenlow – it was p-plain truth.

DORA (*airily*). Mr Copperfield, my little dog Jip has run off.
Would you help me to look for him? I think he may be in the
shrubbery.

She goes off, knowing he is her slave. DAVID *turns to*
AGNES, *whispering urgently.*

DAVID. Such bright eyes, such a delightful voice, such a gay laugh!
She is a goddess, a sylph, a fairy – I don't know what she is!

AGNES *steps forward.*

AGNES. She is waiting for you in the shrubbery! Go on!

DAVID *goes. She laughs.*

Oh, David. Dear, dear David, how lovable you are.

URIAH *appears behind her.*

URIAH. Miss Agnes? Your father –

AGNES. Please, Father... Don't –

URIAH. Mr Wickfield is struggling a little with Dr Strong's
private papers, Miss Agnes. I think it would be better if you
persuaded him to retire to bed. He is considerably – fatigued,
Miss Agnes, and seems easily confused.

AGNES. He cannot do Dr Strong's business now. He must not. He must go to bed. Oh, Uriah, what are we to do?

URIAH. Oh, Miss Agnes. Leave the business with me. Let Mr Wickfield enjoy his claret like a gentleman, Miss Agnes. Leave everything to me.

Scene Twenty

DORA. Papa is not at home, Mr Copperfield. I'm afraid you will have to make do with my poor conversation. I hope you are not disappointed.

DAVID. No – no! Quite the contrary!

DORA. You mean you would be disappointed with Papa?

DAVID. No – yes – Miss Spenlow, please, I am on the rack!

DORA. You do seem a little agitated.

DAVID. Agitated! I am like to die! Surely you must know, Miss Spenlow – Dora! I idolise – I worship – I love you! I love you and I cannot bear it! I have loved you since first I saw you, every minute, night and day. I shall always love you, every minute, to distraction. Lovers have loved before, and lovers will love again; but no lover has ever loved, might, could, or should ever love, more than I love you – my Dora!

DORA. Well! I suppose we should consider ourselves engaged, then.

DAVID. Engaged! Then you have some feeling for me?

DORA. Darling David, didn't you know? Of course I do.

DAVID. Oh, Dora, you have made me the happiest of men. When may I speak to your father?

DORA. My father? Oh, he has only just had me back from Paris. I don't think he is quite ready to lose me, just yet. Let us be secret for a little –

DAVID. You think he won't approve of me?

DORA. I think he will love you – once I have softened him.

DAVID. And until then?

DORA. Until then? My dearest David – do you know, I think that dog has run off again into the shrubbery?

Gazing into each other's eyes, they join hands and go off together. DAVID *immediately bounds back and begins to shout to an absent* AGNES. *He is an inspired adolescent romantic, heedless that he is in a public street.*

Scene Twenty-One

DAVID. Agnes, Agnes, she loves me! We are engaged! Secretly, of course, but not dishonourably: her father will know, when it is time. Engaged! To Dora! She loves me!

STEERFORTH *comes on and stares at him, astonished.*

She loves me! DORA LOVES ME!

STEERFORTH. My God. It's little Copperfield.

DAVID. What? Oh, I do beg your pardon –

STEERFORTH. I see you don't remember me.

DAVID. Steerforth! My dear Steerforth, I never, never, never was so glad.

STEERFORTH. So I have observed. An affair of the heart, I assume. Who would have thought it, little Copperfield?

DAVID. I am overjoyed, Steerforth, to see *you*. What do you do here?

STEERFORTH. My ever-indulgent mama has made me a college man at Oxford. I get bored to death up there, so I have drifted out of town in search of entertainment. Do you know, Copperfield, you are just what you used to be: not altered in the least. Now, tell me, what are you about?

DAVID. Oh, well: I have been adopted by my great aunt, who has given me an education and purchased me a place with a law practice, and I have fallen in love with the daughter of one of the partners – and Steerforth, she will have me! And today, I'm off to share my joyful news with my friends in Yarmouth.

STEERFORTH. What, the quaint and jolly fisherfolk?

DAVID. My special family: Dan Peggotty, his nephew, Ham, and his pretty niece, Emily. Steerforth, if you are seeking entertainment – come with me!

Scene Twenty-Two

The bed returns as the boat-house at Yarmouth.

HAM. Master Davy, bor!

DANIEL. This be the gentleman you've heard on, Emily, Master Davy's friend Mr Steerforth.

STEERFORTH. Now shame upon you, Copperfield. You did not tell me that Mr Peggotty's gentle niece was the brightest sea nymph on Yarmouth's shore.

DANIEL. Gentlemen, you come to see us on the brightest night of my life as ever was or will be. Excuse me for being in a state of mind. I ask your pardon – I'm a boiled shellfish and I can't say more.

HAM. You see, Davy – Mr Steerforth, a certain person that has knowed our Emily from the time when her father was drowndead, seen her a babby, a young girl, a woman – a rough chap, my build, bit of sou'wester in him, salty but honest, on the whole –

DANIEL. This blessed tarpaulin here has gone and lost his heart to our Little Emily. And though she's knowed him all these years, and is as free as a fish to choose for herself, she has said she'll be his wife!

DAVID. Oh, Emily! My hand, Ham! May you both be blessed and happy.

STEERFORTH. My hand, too. Ham and Emily, I give you joy. Mr Peggotty, you are a thoroughly good fellow.

STEERFORTH *moves slightly apart*.

DAVID (*to* EMILY). What more can I wish you, Em, my sometime sweetheart, than a lifetime of the love with Ham, which I have found with my Dora?

EMILY. Thank you, my sweet Davy. I hope your Dora knows the goodness of the heart she has won. It is so good to see you, and your grand friend, Mr Steerforth. Is he very rich?

DAVID *goes to* STEERFORTH.

DAVID. Steerforth?

STEERFORTH. I am quite halfway at sea. Halfway at sea.

DAVID. What is the matter?

STEERFORTH. Why go against the tide? Why not make sail, if the current favours? Ham, I am resolved to buy myself a boat. I would like Mr Peggotty to be her master, and to teach me to be a salty sailor.

Scene Twenty-Three

The boat-house is taken away. BETSEY *approaches* DAVID.

DAVID. Aunt Betsey, what an unexpected pleasure.

BETSEY. David, my dear.

DAVID. Aunt. Listen, I have some wonderful news for you.

BETSEY. Fancy yourself in love, don't you, David?

DAVID. Fancy, Aunt Betsey! I adore her!

BETSEY. She isn't silly, David?

DAVID. We are young and inexperienced, I know –

BETSEY. I fear I have hard news for you. Have you learned to be firm and self-reliant, David?

DAVID. I hope so, yes, Aunt. Why?

BETSEY. David, my love, I'm ruined.

DAVID. What?

BETSEY. I have lost most of everything I have in the world.

DAVID. But how, ruined?

BETSEY. Your old aunt had some property, which on Mr Wickfield's advice, returned good interest. Again on his advice, we looked around for a new investment, and, well, the advice was not so good this time: she lost some here, some there, until –

Enter DICK.

DICK. It has fallen quite to pieces.

BETSEY. I still have the cottage, God be praised... So I am not quite destitute. Wickfield is quite stunned by this outcome. He has put all future business in the hands of Uriah Heep.

DICK. He has made him his partner.

DAVID. Uriah is his partner? And Agnes? What of Agnes?

BETSEY. Agnes must continue to look after her father. I think she must forget the prospect of a good marriage. So, David. That is how we stand. I am sorry, my boy, but your own prospects are quite altered. I fear you must speak seriously with your beloved Dora.

DICK. Come, Mr David. We must act the play out to the end.

DAVID. My God, I have lost her... Dora! I have lost her. Oh, Dora! Dora – I will never desert you!

Scene Twenty-Four

AGNES *and* URIAH *are alone together.*

URIAH. Miss Agnes!

AGNES. Uriah – I must congratulate you.

URIAH. Oh, Miss Agnes, thank you. Thank you! I know you must find this business disagreeable.

AGNES. Disagreeable? Why should I?

URIAH. That one so 'umble should have made himself so indispensable to your papa, that he not only makes me his partner, but surrenders to me all authority for the conduct of the business.

AGNES. Your ascendancy is very great.

URIAH. In truth, Miss Agnes, it is, isn't it? And do you know, I think your papa is a little afraid of me, Miss Agnes? A little afraid of 'umble Uriah!

AGNES. I am sure Papa feels nothing but gratitude.

URIAH. I hope you do not share his fear, Miss Agnes. I would not like to feel repelled by you, or resented by you, that I was uncongenial to you. I may be in a position of power, but I have not changed. My 'umbleness remains as it always was.

AGNES *and* URIAH *exit.*

Scene Twenty-Five

HAM *comes on.*

HAM. Master Davy, bor?

DAVID. Who is that?

HAM. It's me, Master Davy. Ham.

DAVID. Why, what brings you all the way from Yarmouth, Ham? We're a long way from the sea, here. Has something happened to Peggotty, or your Uncle Dan?

HAM. No, they're well… Master Davy, yon gentleman acquaintance of yourn, Mr Steerforth – would you know where he might be, just now?

DAVID. Steerforth? No. I haven't seen him since we came to visit you. Why?

HAM. It's Little Emily. My love, the hope and pride of my heart, that I would die for – she's gone.

DAVID. 'Gone'? What do you mean, 'gone'?

HAM. She's run off, Davy, bor. Emily's run off with your Mr Steerforth.

End of Act One.

ACT TWO

Scene Twenty-Six

The STEERFORTH *family home*. MRS STEERFORTH, DAVID *and* DANIEL.

MRS STEERFORTH. I know, with deep regret, what has brought you here. What do you want of me?

DANIEL. Mrs Steerforth, your son has done my niece a great wrong. He did so by promising to make her a lady. I come to know, ma'am, if he will keep his word.

MRS STEERFORTH. He will not.

DANIEL. Why not?

MRS STEERFORTH. It is impossible. He would disgrace himself.

DAVID. Mrs Steerforth! He disgraces himself if he does not.

MRS STEERFORTH. You cannot fail to know that she is far below him.

DANIEL. Raise her up.

MRS STEERFORTH. She is uneducated and ignorant.

DANIEL. Teach her better.

MRS STEERFORTH. Since you oblige me to speak plainly – her humble connections render such a thing impossible.

DANIEL. Hark to this, ma'am. Save her from this disgrace, and she shall never be disgraced by us. Not one of us, her family, will trouble your great house. We'll be content to think of her from far off. We'll be content to trust her to her husband, and bide the time when all of us shall be alike in quality afore our God.

MRS STEERFORTH. I repeat, it is impossible. Such a marriage would irretrievably blight my son's career and ruin his prospects. Nothing is more certain than it can never take place. If there is any other compensation –

DANIEL. I am looking at the likeness of a face that has looked at me in my own home, smiling and friendly, when it was so treacherous. If the likeness of that face don't turn to burning fire, at the thought of offering money for my child's blight and ruin, it is as bad. I don't know, being a lady's, but what it's worse.

MRS STEERFORTH. What compensation can you make to me for opening such a pit between me and my son? What can your love be, to mine? My son, who has been the object of my life, whose every wish I have gratified, from whom I have no separate existence – to take up in a moment with a miserable girl, and to quit me for her! Is this no injury? Let him put his whim away, and he is welcome back. Let him not put her away, now, and he shall never more come near me. This is the separation that has been made between us. And is this no injury?

DANIEL. I come here with no hope, and I take away no hope. I have done what I thought should be done, but I never looked for any good to come. Master Davy, I'm going to seek her. I'm going to seek my niece, wherever she has been taken. If any hurt should come to me, the last words I leave for her are these: 'My unchanged love is with my darling child, and I forgive her.' God bless you, Master Davy, better fortune – and better friends – attend you.

DANIEL *goes*.

MRS STEERFORTH. This is a fellow, Mr Copperfield, to champion and bring here.

DAVID. He is a deeply injured man, Mrs Steerforth.

MRS STEERFORTH. I would trample on the whole worthless set. I would have his house pulled down. I would have her branded on the face and dressed in rags, and cast on to the streets to starve. I would see it done. I would do it myself. You traitor!

MRS STEERFORTH *sweeps off*.

DAVID. Oh, Emily. How have you been deceived. How could you do it, Steerforth? You called yourself my friend. Oh, where may I turn now? Parted from fortune, friends and family, my own beloved removed beyond my reach?

Scene Twenty-Seven

URIAH. Master Copperfield! To see you brought low is something I never expected. But things happen which we never can expect: such things have happened to me, in my 'umble station, that it seems to rain blessings on my head, Master Copperfield – sorry, *Mister* Copperfield.

DAVID. Uriah!

URIAH. I am rejoiced to see you, Mr Copperfield, even under your present circumstances. But, Mr Copperfield, it isn't money makes the man. I am unequal with my 'umble powers to express what it is, but it isn't money.

DAVID. Friendship perhaps? True friendship? Friendship which has no regard for pride of place or the size of a purse?

URIAH. Well, Master David, you are sufficiently exalted in your person to understand such friendship. A lowly person like myself cannot say. But here I have an old friend of yours, who shares your admirable sentiments.

Enter MICAWBER.

DAVID. Mr Micawber!

MICAWBER. Why, is it possible – Mr Copperfield? My dear sir, this is a meeting calculated to impress the mind with a sense of the instability and uncertainty of all human endeavour – in short, it is most extraordinary. My dear fellow, how do you do?

DAVID. I thought you were in Plymouth, Mr Micawber.

MICAWBER. We were in – Plymouth, yes. But my talent was not suited to the Plymouth custom house. In consequence I turned my eye to the Medway coal trade, only to discover, not only did that excellent business need talent, it needed capital. However, my young friend, you find me established now, on a small and unassuming scale, here in Canterbury.

DAVID. Mr Heep is your employer?

URIAH. Yes, indeed, Master Copperfield. Indeed, it was on hearing the fulsomeness with which he expressed your sentiments on friendship, that I took him into my employ.

MICAWBER (*confidentially*). I'll tell you what, my dear young friend, your friend Heep might make Attorney General. If I had known that young man at the period of my budgetary crisis, all I can say is, I believe my creditors would have been a great deal better managed. He takes my debts and settles them, against my future emolument in his service.

DAVID. I understand there has been a change in *your* expectations, Uriah...

URIAH. Ah! No doubt Miss Agnes has intimated something of the business to you. I am glad that she has noted it. And what a prophet it has proved you to be, Master Copperfield. Don't you remember saying once that I might become Mr Wickfield's partner?

DAVID. I remember, though I'm sure I didn't think it likely.

URIAH. And do you remember, Master Copperfield, how you said that everyone must admire Miss Agnes? How I thanked you for it! For you kindled the sparks of ambition in my 'umble breast, and the 'umblest of persons may be the instruments of good. I hope I may be such an instrument to Mr Wickfield. How imprudent he has been.

DAVID. Imprudent, Uriah?

URIAH. Thank you, thank you, Master Copperfield! To hear you say 'Uriah' – it's like the blowing of old breezes. Greatly imprudent. If anyone else had been in my place during the

last few years, he would by now have Mr Wickfield quite
under his thumb: quite un-der-his-thumb. There would have
been a loss. There would have been disgrace. Mr Wickfield
knows it... May I make a little confidence to you, Master
Copperfield? Miss Agnes –

DAVID. Miss Agnes, Uriah?

URIAH. Oh, how pleasant to be called 'Uriah', spontaneously!
Oh, Master Copperfield, with what pure affection do I love
the ground my Agnes walks on.

DAVID. Does Agnes –

URIAH. My Agnes!

DAVID. Does your – Does she – Have you made your feelings
known to her?

URIAH. Oh no! Oh, dear me, no! Not to anyone but you. I am
only just emerging from my lowliness. I rest my hope on her
observing how useful I am to her father, how I smooth the
way for him, and keep him straight. And that she may come,
on his account, to be kind to me. And if you will have the
goodness to keep my secret, and not in general, to go against
me, I shall take it as a particular favour. You see, Master
Copperfield, where a person loves, a person is a little jealous.

DAVID. You are not still jealous of me, are you?

URIAH. No, Master Copperfield, I know that your affection is
that of, say, a brother, or cousin.

DAVID. Cousin?

URIAH. Like Mrs Strong's cousin Jack Maldon, that lives with
the doctor and his pretty little wife. Always with her on her
visits, ordering and shoving me about! Now, I don't like that
sort of thing. No, I don't. I'm not going to let myself be run
down. Not before my Agnes. I ain't going to be plotted
against.

DAVID. No one plots against you.

URIAH. I mustn't be put upon, Master Copperfield. I can't
allow people in my way, and I won't. I have felt it incumbent
upon me, Master Copperfield, to point out to Dr Strong the
goings-on between his wife and Mr Gentleman Jack Maldon.
That everyone who has seen them knows Maldon and the
doctor's wife are sweet on one another. She only married
Strong for his money, and when he dies she'll marry her
cousin as fast as she can.

DAVID. My God. You villain!

*DAVID strikes URIAH's cheek. URIAH catches DAVID's
hand and holds it beside his face.*

MICAWBER. Copperfield!

DAVID. You dog.

URIAH. Don't say that. I know you'll be sorry afterwards.

He begins to lower DAVID's arm.

I always liked you, Copperfield, and I forgive you.

DAVID. You forgive me?

URIAH. I do. I always liked you, and will be a friend to you. In
spite of yourself.

He shakes DAVID's lifeless hand.

Now you know what you've got to expect. Come, Micawber,
Mr Wickfield's business is waiting for us.

MICAWBER. Mr Copperfield, have you taken leave of your
senses? I am greatly indebted to Mr Heep. I hold a position
of trust with Mr Heep. Any action, sentiment or acquaintance
incompatible with that function, I cannot entertain. I therefore take the liberty of drawing a line in our friendly inter-
course. I trust I give no offence.

MICWABER and URIAH exit.

Scene Twenty-Eight

AGNES *comes on.*

DAVID. Is there nothing to be done?

AGNES. There is God to trust in.

DAVID. Agnes – you know how much I love you, how much I owe you. As I know how much you love your father and would spare him from misfortune. Please, Agnes, assure me: you will never sacrifice yourself to a mistaken sense of duty, will you...? Say you have no such thought, Agnes!

AGNES. You must attend to your own troubles, David. Your aunt's ill-fortune, your current circumstances – and your Dora.

DAVID. But you are my sister!

AGNES. No, David. I am not. You must remember that. I am not your sister. We are not family. There are others who are, whose protection must be your first duty. Our family demands our first duty, and my duty must be to my father.

DAVID. Then what must I do?

AGNES. Write to Dora's father. Relate plainly all that has taken place. Ask their permission to visit. Accept any condition he imposes. Do nothing secret and clandestine. Trust to your fidelity and openness – and to Dora.

DAVID. I will, Agnes. As I will ever trust your good advice. Heaven bless you.

Scene Twenty-Nine

DAVID *and* DORA *are married. Tableau.* AGNES *is seen to encourage* DORA. *The bed is brought on and* DAVID *and* DORA *end up in bed together asleep. They wake the next day.*

DORA. Well? Are you happy now, you foolish boy? Are you sure you don't repent?

DAVID. I am happy now. And amazed. You are always here. I don't have to scheme constantly for opportunities to be alone with you. I can't get over that we are alone together as a matter of course, no one to please but one another, and one another to please – for life.

DORA. For life – that sounds very serious.

DAVID. It is serious. And we must be serious about it, sometimes.

DORA. You're going to scold me.

DAVID. No, I'm not, my sweet! I'm only going to reason.

DORA. Oh! Reasoning is worse than scolding. I didn't marry to be reasoned with. (*She becomes flirtatiously petulant.*) If you meant to reason with such a poor little thing as I am, you ought to have told me so, you cruel boy.

DAVID. Dora, my darling –

DORA. No. I am not your darling. Because you must be sorry you married me, if all you want to do is reason with me.

They embrace. Enter a sullen servant, MARY ANNE PARAGON.

MARY ANNE. Your dinner's out. (*She exits.*)

DAVID. Dear life! That woman's sense of time! I think you must speak to her, my dear.

DORA. Oh no. Please, I couldn't.

DAVID. But why ever not?

DORA. Because I am such a little goose, and she knows it.

A SOLDIER *appears from under the bed.* DORA *calls out to* MARY ANNE.

Mary Anne! There's a soldier under the bed!

MARY ANNE. My cousin, ma'am. He's visiting.

DORA. Mary Anne! He's eating our dinner!

MARY ANNE. That's right, ma'am. He'll be gone tomorrow.

DORA. Mary Anne! The soldier's wrapping the silver up in the bedsheets!

MARY ANNE. That's right, ma'am. We're taking them to the cleaners!

Exit MARY ANNE *and the* SOLDIER.

DORA. Mary Anne! Mary Anne? Mary Anne?

DAVID. They've disappeared? With the silverware and the bedlinen?

DORA. Oh, I don't know what to do. Everyone we have anything to do with seems to cheat us. If I go in a shop, it's a signal for the damaged goods to be brought out. If I buy a lobster, it's full of water. If I buy meat, it's sure to be tough. If I send clothes to the washerwoman, she pawns them!

DAVID. Perhaps we are to blame for not learning how to cope.

DORA. Now you are going to be cross.

DAVID. No, no. Let me explain what I mean. We lose money and comfort, and sometimes our good temper, by not learning to be more careful. I fear these people turn out ill, because we don't turn out very well ourselves.

DORA. Did you ever see me take gold watches?

DAVID. What? Who said anything about gold watches?

DORA. You did. You said I hadn't turned out well, and you compared me to him!

DAVID. Who?

DORA. The kitchen boy.

DAVID. What?

DORA. The kitchen boy. The kitchen boy has stolen my gold
watch. (*She bursts into tears*.) Oh, David. What a dreadful
wife I am to you. What am I going to do? I am quite dizzy.
Oh, whatever am I going to do!

Scene Thirty

DAVID (*to* BETSEY). Heaven knows, Aunt, I don't mean to be
unreasonable.

BETSEY. You must have patience, David.

DAVID. You don't think you could advise and counsel Dora
now and then?

BETSEY. No. Never ask me such a thing. David – you have
chosen a very pretty and a very affectionate child to be your
wife. Estimate her by the qualities she has, and not by the
qualities she does not. If you can foster new qualities in her,
so much the better. If you cannot, then accustom yourself to
do without. But your future is between you two. No one can
assist you. You must work it out for yourselves. This is
marriage, David, and heaven bless you in it, for you are a
pair of babes in the wood together.

Scene Thirty-One

DORA. My love, I am very sorry. These accounts make my head swim. Will you try to teach me?

DAVID. If all I succeed in is giving you headaches, I must teach myself first to be a gentler teacher.

DORA. But you can learn. You are a clever, clever man. I know I am just a child. Still, you know your foolish child-wife loves you.

DAVID. Child-wife?

DORA. Mmm. Loves you. Do you love her?

DAVID. Indeed I do.

They kiss. DORA*'s hand goes to her head.* MICAWBER *appears with a letter.*

Scene Thirty-Two

MICAWBER. 'From Wilkins Micawber, Canterbury, to Mr David Copperfield: My Dear Sir, I can walk no more erect before my fellow man. The worm is at its work, and will soon dispose of its victim. The sooner the better. Placed in a mental position of peculiar painfulness, beyond the assuaging reach even of Mrs Micawber's influence...'

He mumbles on. MRS MICAWBER *appears with another letter.*

MRS MICAWBER. 'Dear Mr Copperfield: You will doubtless be surprised to receive this communication. Mr Micawber is entirely changed. He is reserved. He is secret. The pecuniary means of meeting our expenses are obtained from him with the greatest difficulty. Mr Micawber is morose. He is severe. He is estranged.'

MICAWBER. An ability exists on my part of wielding the thunderbolt, of directing the devouring and avenging flame, before I take leave of my sea of troubles for ever.

DAVID. Wielding the thunderbolt and directing the avenging flame? Micawber, what are you about?

MICAWBER. I shall be outside the south wall of the King's Bench Prison, the day after tomorrow, at seven in the evening.

MICAWBER *strikes seven on the rails of the bed.*

DAVID. Mr Micawber?

MICAWBER. Mr Copperfield.

DAVID. You are in low spirits.

MICAWBER. I am, sir.

DAVID. What is the matter, my friend?

MICAWBER. Your friend? You recall me to my former self, Mr Copperfield. What is the matter? Villainy. Baseness. Deception, fraud, conspiracy are the matter – and the name of the whole matter is Uriah Heep. Ah! The struggle is over! I will lead this life no more!

DAVID. Please, Mr Micawber!

MICAWBER. No more! Mr Copperfield, I have a secret, and I will expose the intolerable ruffian. I am upon his track. Meet me this day-week and see me bring him down. Bring your esteemed aunt, Betsey Trotwood. Know, Heep, I will lead this life no more! (*He leaves with an impressive flourish.*)

Scene Thirty-Three

DORA *sitting on the bed, struggling with an account book.*

DORA. Do you think navy rum a ladylike drink?

DAVID. Not in the least.

DORA. Or gin with porter?

DAVID. Good God, no. Why do you ask?

DORA. Well, I've been trying to keep up with the housekeeping accounts, and I find things like, 'A quart of navy rum to Mrs Copperfield, Monday.'

DAVID. Let me see. 'A quart of gin and cloves to Mrs Copperfield, Wednesday. Two quarts rum and peppermint, Mrs Copperfield, Thursday. Twelve bottles porter, Mrs Copperfield, Friday' – A quart of navy rum? Twelve bottles of porter? For you, Dora?

DORA. That's what it says, dearest.

DAVID. I think we must look for a new cook, my sweet.

DORA. I *thought* she was very cheerful, these last few days. Oh, dear. I'm afraid I'll never learn to be wise. You must be cross with me.

DAVID. No. I love you.

DORA. But I wanted to be wise. For you. I know you try to make me wise.

DAVID. That's my conceit. I'll try no more. I love you just the way you are.

They kiss. He spins her round.

DORA. Oh, set me down, David.

DAVID. I'm sorry, have I made you dizzy?

DORA. Yes, you have. Either you – or the navy rum!

The bed is removed.

Scene Thirty-Four

MRS STEERFORTH *and* DANIEL *are in conversation.*

MRS STEERFORTH. The girl has been found?

DANIEL. When my Em'ly was a child, she used to talk about
the sea, and them coasts where it was dark blue and shining
in the sun. I knowed in my mind he would take her to those
countries. I knowed he'd have told her the wonders of them,
and how she was to be a lady there. I went across-channel to
France, and followed upon their path through Switzerland
and Italy. I found her there, deserted by your son. I gave her
my forgiveness, and I brought her home.

MRS STEERFORTH. And my son?

DANIEL. Your son is nowt to me, now that I have my Emily
once more. I understand he has a taste for the seafaring I
taught him, and is now a-coasting Spain.

MRS STEERFORTH. And now I am to see James Steerforth's
fancy?

DANIEL. She wishes you to know her innocent and abused,
ma'am. And that she sought no disaffection between your
son and you.

Enter EMILY.

MRS STEERFORTH. He was a poor creature to be taken in by
that mock-modesty and hanging head.

EMILY. When you know what I have suffered, and how I am
fallen, you may yet show me some compassion, ma'am.

MRS STEERFORTH. Do you know what you have done? Did
you ever think of the home you have laid waste?

EMILY. Was there night or day when I did not think of my
home?

MRS STEERFORTH. Your home! Do you imagine I bestow a
thought upon your home? You were a part of the trade in

your home, and bought and sold like any other thing your people dealt in.

EMILY. Don't visit my disgrace and shame on folks who are as honourable as you. Have some respect for them, as you are a lady, though you have no mercy for me.

MRS STEERFORTH. I speak of his home. Are you a worthy cause of division between a lady and her son, of grief in a house where you wouldn't be admitted as a kitchen girl?

EMILY. Until I met your son I had been brought up as virtuous as you or any lady. I was going to be the wife of as good a man as any gentleman. When your son wearied of me, ma'am, he left me on pretence of returning in a day or so, then wrote proposing I should marry his manservant. When I refused this dishonourable course, I was held by force. And when I escaped, it was poor folk who aided me, not for the reward they might seek from a lady, but because they knew I had been a boatman's daughter. Ma'am, you must know your son, and his power over a weak, vain girl – a power he used to deceive me. You must know that I believed him, trusted him and loved him.

MRS STEERFORTH *strikes blindly at* EMILY. *She misses, and stands frozen, her hand in mid-air.*

MRS STEERFORTH. You love him? You? I was curious to see what such a thing as you is like. I am satisfied. I had thought you a broken toy that had lasted its time and been thrown away. But, no – you are a very lady, an ill-used innocent, with a fresh heart full of love and trustfulness. I cannot breathe the air you breathe. Therefore I will have it cleared and purified. If you seek refuge in this town, or any other within my reach, in any character but that of your disgrace, I will have you proclaimed as a common drab and a practised deceiver. I understand they whip such creatures.

DANIEL. My God, what would you have her do?

MRS STEERFORTH. Do? Live in her reflections. Consecrate her existence to the recollection of James Steerforth's tenderness. He would have made her wife to his serving-man.

MRS STEERFORTH *goes.*

EMILY. Oh, Uncle!

DANIEL. She cannot hurt you, child, she cannot hurt you. She loves her son, and she cannot bear what she has made him, or to look upon his handiwork. Come, Emily. Let us go home.

Scene Thirty-Five

HAM. Master Davy, bor?

DAVID. Why, it's Ham! What news, Ham – is Emily safe?

HAM. Aye, she is safe.

DAVID. Where is she?

HAM. With Uncle Dan in Yarmouth. For now.

DAVID. 'For now'?

HAM. Aye. Uncle Dan – he has reckoned that there is no future for us in England, Master Davy. Emily is shunned by folks in Yarmouth, now. That man's mother – she is cruel unforgiving, and she has much influence. Uncle Dan reckons the future lies over the sea. In a place where Emily can meet no reproach. He is planning for a new life in Australia.

DAVID. I am to lose you all, then, just as the family is made one again.

HAM. No, Master Davy. Not all. I'm a-staying.

DAVID. Oh, but Ham –

HAM. It ain't that I don't forgive her. I have done that, with all my heart. Truth is, I hardly blamed her. And that's it, I reckon. I blame myself, for having pressed my affections on her. If I hadn't had her promise to marry, and we'd still been in our old friendly way, maybe she would have told me she was tempted – and maybe I might have saved her. And now – I loved her – I loved her too deep. I can only be happy by forgetting what might have been with her, what never can be now. So – when they take ship for their new life, I stop in Yarmouth.

DAVID *takes* HAM *by the hand. They embrace.*

DAVID. Ham, my friend, you are a true man. Any comfort I can give, any service I can render – it is yours for the asking. You understand that?

HAM. I'll take my leave. They take ship in six weeks, Master Davy. Will you give Em this letter, when you take your farewell?

DAVID. Won't you see her yourself?

HAM. I have thought of it, and it's best I don't.

DAVID (*embracing* HAM *once more*). I'll come to Yarmouth, Ham, when they are gone. Until then.

HAM. Till then.

They part and exit.

Scene Thirty-Six

DORA *walking slowly, with* BETSEY *supporting her.*

BETSEY. Of course you feel tired, my darling, but in a few days you will be well again, and running about as you used to. In the meantime you must suffer to be pampered and waited on by those that love you.

DORA. I am being a silly little thing.

BETSEY. No, you are not. Shall we sit you here? Yes?

DORA. You will wear yourself out with all this fuss.

BETSEY. Now, my little blossom, fussing over you is the merriest thing in our dull workaday lives. You must let us have our fun. It is only for a little time.

DORA. Where is David?

BETSEY. He is preventing Mr Micawber from disturbing your rest. Micawber wishes me to attend at his exposure of Uriah Heep's villainy. He is downstairs practising his heroic indignation. I've warned David that if he tries to do away with himself, he's to keep the blood off the carpets.

DORA. I think Micawber is fun, Aunt Betsey. You must go with him to witness his struggle with Heep.

BETSEY. Heep? What have I to do with Uriah Heep? Let someone go in my stead. I cannot leave you, to entertain the fantasies of your theatrical Micawber.

Enter DAVID.

DAVID. Forgive me. Aunt Betsey – it is Micawber. He wishes us to go with him without delay. The man is somewhat agitated. He is promising to erupt like a human Vesuvius.

BETSEY. Then you must ask Mr Micawber to delay his volcanic activities till he is out of the house.

DORA. If you don't go to see the fun, Aunt, I shall lead you such a life. I shall tease you, and make myself so disagreeable, you'll wish you'd gone and never come back. And I'm not really ill – not really ill.

Scene Thirty-Seven

URIAH *is brought on, sitting on top of the bedframe, using a trunk as a desk.* DAVID, BETSEY, DICK *and* MICAWBER *join* AGNES *and confront* URIAH: *he descends to meet them.*

URIAH. Well, this is indeed an unexpected pleasure – all such friends at once is a treat unlooked for! Mr Copperfield, I hope I see you well, sir, and – if I may 'umbly express myself so – friendly towards them as is ever your friends. Don't wait, Micawber. I hope Mrs Copperfield is getting better – we have been made quite uneasy here by the poor accounts we have had of her lately, I assure you. Don't wait, Micawber. And Miss Trotwood! Things are changed in this office, Miss Trotwood, since I was but an 'umble clerk, but I am not changed, oh no, ma'am. I am not changed. Don't wait, Micawber. (*To* DICK.) This gentleman, I'm afraid, is new to my acquaintance – Micawber? What are you waiting for – I told you not to wait. Did you not hear me?

MICAWBER. Yes.

URIAH. Then why do you wait?

MICAWBER. I choose to wait.

URIAH. Go along! I shall have to talk to him.

MICAWBER. If there is a *scoundrel* on this earth, with whom I have already talked too much, that scoundrel's name is – *Heep*!

URIAH (*recovering from the shock*). O-ho, I see, this is a conspiracy. You have met here by appointment. Now have a care, Copperfield, you'll make nothing of this. We understand each other, you and me. There's no love between us. You always were a proud puppy, and you envy me my rise, don't you? Plot against me and I'll plot against you! Micawber – be off! I'll talk to *you* presently.

DICK. I see a sudden change in this fellow. Extraordinary.

DAVID. Mr Micawber – deal with him as he deserves.

URIAH. You are a precious set, ain't you? Buying my clerk to defame me with lies. My clerk is scum! As you were, Copperfield, before you took Miss Trotwood's charity. Miss Trotwood, have a care. You might be poorer still, by one who knows too well your stock of savings. I won't know your story professionally for nothing, old lady! Miss Wickfield: if you love your father, don't join this gang against me. I'll ruin him if you do. Now come! I have some of you under the harrow. Think twice before it goes over you. Micawber! I will crush you!

DICK. A remarkable change.

MICAWBER. If you please, Mr Copperfield.

> MRS MICAWBER *revealed at* URIAH*'s 'desk', guarding the evidence with a wooden ruler.*

I appear before you to denounce the most consummate *villain* that has ever existed. I ask no consideration for myself, the victim, from my cradle of pecuniary liabilities; and who by them was driven into the service of this – *Heep* – *Heep* and only *Heep*, is the mainspring of that machine. *Heep* and only *Heep* is the forger and the cheat.

> MRS MICAWBER *hands* DAVID *a document.*
> MICAWBER *takes the ruler from* MRS MICAWBER.

URIAH. What the devil is that, sir?

DAVID. It makes me the agent and friend of Mr Wickfield, Mr Heep. It gives me his power of attorney, to act for him in all matters.

URIAH. He has drunk himself into a state of dotage. This has been got from him by fraud.

DAVID. Most certainly, something has been got from him by fraud. If you please, Mr Micawber.

URIAH. The devil take you!

> *He tries to snatch the document.* MICAWBER *whacks him on the knuckles with the ruler.*

MICAWBER. Approach me again, you *Heep* of infamy, and if
your head is human, I'll break it. Come on, then! (*He holds
the ruler like a sabre*.) No? Then let us continue. *Heep* –
drew me inexorably into a web of emoluments and advances
secured by IOUs and other legal instruments, till I depended
entirely on his blighting favour. As I dwindled, peaked and
pined, he began to use me in the falsification of business and
the mystification of Mr Wickfield. However: when the
contest within myself between stipend and no stipend,
groceries and no groceries, existence and non-existence,
ceased – I took advantage of my opportunities to discover
and expose the major malpractices committed. First – Heep
designedly perplexed and complicated the whole of our
transacted business, induced Mr Wickfield to empower him
to draw sums from certain trustfunds, to meet pretended
charges, and gave it the appearance of Mr Wickfield's
dishonesty.

URIAH. This is fanciful imagination –

MICAWBER. Second – Heep has systematically forged, to
various entries, books and documents, the signature of Mr
Wickfield. In my possession is this pocketbook, a pocketbook in which this – *Heep* – practised his imitations of Mr
Wickfield's signature.

URIAH. There is no pocketbook.

MICAWBER (*handing* DICK *a pocketbook*). There is. Rescued
from the office stove. Third and last – By falsifying
accounts, by pretended borrowings at high interest, Heep
induced Mr Wickfield into a belief in impending bankruptcy,
from which only Heep could save him. In exchange for
which, Mr Wickfield relinquished his share of the
partnership and placed himself entirely in the hands of the
very man who had accomplished his destruction. THAT
MAN IS HEEP. I can substantiate all these accusations. Let
my debts o'erwhelm me, let me sink beneath that flood with
my ill-starred family. It may reasonably be supposed that the
baby will be the first to expire, that the twins will follow

next. So be it! I ask no more. Let it be, in justice, merely said of me, as of a certain naval hero, that what I have done, I did, for England, home, and beauty.

DICK. These signatures are very good. I should like to read your forged account books, Mr Heep.

URIAH. What do you want?

DICK. Restoration, I think. Of everything owed to Miss Trotwood, and to Mr Wickfield. Yes – restoration.

DAVID. To the last farthing.

URIAH. I must have time to think.

DICK. Certainly, certainly. You must think, Mr Heep. But until everything is done to our satisfaction, we will keep these wonderful accounts, and – um – the key to the safe, and you must keep to your room, you know, and communicate with no one.

URIAH. I won't do it.

DICK. Then it's Maidstone Jail for you, Mr Heep. Mr Copperfield, will you go and fetch a couple of officers? Come, come, Mr Heep. You know as well as I, you are finished.

URIAH. Copperfield! Stop. Enough. You shall have what you want.

DICK. Let us study the accounts together, sir.

MICAWBER. Gentlemen!

They all push URIAH *into the trunk.*

URIAH (*inside trunk*). Copperfield! I have always hated you. You're an upstart and you've always been against me. And you, Micawber – I'll pay you!

MICAWBER *pushes down lid,* DICK *sits on it. The bed is pushed off upstage.*

Scene Thirty-Eight

MICAWBER. My love!

MRS MICAWBER. I will never desert you!

MICAWBER. I never thought you would!

AGNES. Praise be to God, we are saved.

BETSEY. My property, my savings, may be recovered?

DAVID. Mr Micawber, you shall fear poverty no longer. You have us all in your debt and we shall not let you sink.

MICAWBER. Why, what care I for riches! I am restored to the confidence of my Emma! The veil that interposed between us is withdrawn. Now welcome poverty, welcome misery, houselessness, hunger, rags and beggary! Our mutual love sustains us to the end!

DAVID. Amen to that, Mr Micawber, but you'll find there is no need –

MICAWBER (*heedless of* DAVID). My Emma! My life!

AGNES. Forgive me, I must tell my father that the cloud is lifted from our lives.

DAVID. Of course. And I must go to Dora.

BETSEY. Run and tell her, David.

AGNES. Tell her I will call tonight.

DAVID. Oh, Aunt, Agnes is safe. I feared for her so. Uriah – well, it is over. And your losses may be recovered, and – oh, what a tale we have for Dora. What a tale we have for little Dora!

DAVID *goes*.

BETSEY (*to* AGNES). Don't wait for me. I wish to have a word with this extraordinary Mr Micawber.

AGNES *goes*.

My nephew has told me the history of your past tribulations, and I know too well that your present heroism on behalf of others has precipitated fresh crisis. My nephew has also told me of the intention of some of his acquaintance to seek a new life, and renewed opportunity, in Australia. And it occurred to me, Mr Micawber... I wonder you have never turned your own thoughts to emigration.

MICAWBER. Madam, it was the dream of my youth, and the fallacious aspiration of my riper years.

BETSEY. Why, what a thing it would be for yourself and your family if you were to emigrate now.

MICAWBER (*gloomily*). Capital, madam, capital. I have no capital.

BETSEY. Capital? But you have done us a great service, and what could we do for you, that would be half so good as to find for you the capital?

MICAWBER. I could not possibly accept such a gift.

BETSEY. No?

MICAWBER. No. However... if a sufficient sum could be advanced, say at five per cent interest per annum, upon my personal liability – say my notes of hand, at twelve, eighteen and twenty-four months, respectively, to allow time for something to turn up –

BETSEY. Could be advanced? Can be – shall be, on any terms –

MICAWBER. We could sail with the friends of Mr Copperfield. We might be of assistance and support to one another. Australia...

MRS MICAWBER. A question arises: are the circumstances of Australia such, that a man of Mr Micawber's abilities would have a fair chance of rising in the social scale? I will not say, aspire to be Governor –

BETSEY. No better opening anywhere for a man who conducts himself well and is industrious.

MRS MICAWBER. 'Conducts himself well, and is industrious'? It is evident to me that, for Mr Micawber, the legitimate sphere of action is nowhere else but Australia.

MICAWBER. Under these circumstances it is the land, the only land, for myself and my family. Madam, I accept. Come, my life, let us fix our gaze on the far horizon, and prepare to launch our frail canoe on the ocean of enterprise. Madam, we take our leave.

The MICAWBERS *sweep off.* DAVID *and* AGNES *gently push the bed on.*

BETSEY. Agnes, my dear.

She notices DAVID *is in a state of shock.*

My boy?

AGNES. Dora is very unwell, Miss Trotwood.

DAVID. The doctor said, 'a few days more'. I thought at first he meant till she was well again.

BETSEY, DAVID *and* AGNES *stare into the bed as if* DORA *were there.* DORA *runs on gaily, and skips about the stage. The others are very still and remote from her.*

DORA. Oh, Aunt Betsey! You have your house in Dover again! I wish I'd seen you there with Davy, chasing donkeys and flying kites! David, you never showed me Yarmouth and the Peggotty's boat-house and the bottle place you worked in and the horrible school and where you were born. Remember the places where we were a silly couple and met and walked and talked in secret, and pretended to look for my dog in the shrubbery? What happy days we had together! Such happy days, we'll never forget them.

DAVID. I'll never forget them. Those happy days. We pretended to look for her dog in the shrubbery.

DORA. You must think me a child again, but I don't care, I'm going to run and skip and be a silly child-wife for ever. I am so happy, I'll never grow up!

DAVID. I have tried to resign myself. To console myself. But what I cannot settle is that the end must come. I hold her hand in mine, still. I hold her heart in mine. I see her love for me, alive in all its strength.

AGNES. She wasn't born to be old, David, my dear.

DORA. If the years had worn on, you would have wearied of me, still a child-wife. I would have been less and less a companion for you. I would never have changed or improved. You know it. And I know it. It's best this way. (*She starts to leave*.)

DAVID. Dora!

But she has gone.

BETSEY. Oh, my boy. I am so sorry.

DAVID *is left alone. Blackout*.

Scene Thirty-Nine

Lights up on the MICAWBERS, *dressed for the sea voyage in over-the-top oilskins,* MICAWBER *with a telescope. Quantities of luggage*.

MICAWBER. The luxuries of the old country we abandon. In the Land of the Free, the denizens of the forest cannot expect to participate in refinement.

DAVID. I hope to hear from you, Mr Micawber, whenever you have the opportunity of writing.

MICAWBER. Please heaven, there will be many opportunities. Porpoises and dolphins, I believe, will be frequently observed athwart our bows, and either on starboard or larboard, objects of interest will continually be descried. In short, I will write.

The bed arrives bedecked with bunting and a lifebelt on the front. A SAILOR *takes one of the boards and puts it down as a gangplank. The* MICAWBERS *start to board*.

MRS MICAWBER. We shall not forget the parent tree when our race attains eminence and fortune. We shall recall Britannia.

MICAWBER. I am bound to say, my dear, Britannia has never done much for me, and calling her to mind may not be my first wish.

MRS MICAWBER. You do not know your power, Micawber. Enough of delay. Enough of disappointment. Enough of limited means. That was the old country. This is the new. Produce your reparation. It is mine. And, Mr Micawber – wielding the rod of talent and of power in Australia, will you be nothing in England? You will be a page in history!

MICAWBER. My love, it is impossible not to be touched by your affection. I will defer to your good sense. What will be – will be. And heaven forbid I should grudge my native country a portion of my wealth.

AGNES *and* BETSEY *hurry on.*

AGNES. Every blessing and success attend you.

BETSEY. My love goes with both of you.

DAVID. I was afraid we would miss you.

DANIEL *and* EMILY *enter. She boards the boat silently.*

DANIEL (*produces a legal paper*). Mr Micawber? There's a paper for you, sir.

MICAWBER. Thank you, sir. (*Reads paper.*) Aah! Where is my knife! Where is the rail, that I may cast myself overboard! Look at this document – '*Heep versus Micawber*'! Even now he reclaims the debts he trapped me into! Am I to see, after all, my family cast into the parish workhouse?

DANIEL. No, sir. 'Tis paid.

MICAWBER. 'Paid'?

DANIEL. Aye, sir. I settled it with the officer. I reckoned you would not wish to be hindered with such business at this time. I give it you, that no man may claim it is unsettled.

BETSEY. Well done, Mr Peggotty!

DAVID. Mr Peggotty, I have a letter for you. Let me make up the sum.

MICAWBER. Sir, you overwhelm me. I am for ever in your debt, and I hope, for ever your friend.

MRS MICAWBER. Oh, Wilkins, I will never desert you!

DANIEL. Well, Master Davy. Time for the last word. Ham's letter, I will give our Emily once we have sailed. Emily begs you not to seek her now, but to remember her as she was when you were children. She says, she prays for you in your own sorrow, and will do so till she dies. And asks you take her blessing. As I give you mine, afore we parts.

DAVID. Heaven bless you. You are the best of men.

DANIEL. Your hand, Master Davy, then we are gone. Farewell. Farewell, all. And farewell, England.

DANIEL boards the ship. The SAILOR *starts to pull the ship off.*

MICAWBER. To the new life!

ALL. The new life!

Tableau, as for a photograph. All sing lustily 'Abide With Me'. Then the stage clears, except for DAVID *and* AGNES.

DAVID. God bless them all.

AGNES. And God bless you, David.

DAVID. Oh, Agnes – they are gone for ever, and I alone am left behind. I know of another lonely heart. My mind runs constantly on him – Ham, in his misery and solitude. I think I will go down to Yarmouth.

Scene Forty

A group of oilskin-clad figures on a storm-lashed beach.

MAN 1. Where is she? Where is she?

MAN 2. There! There!

MAN 1. Heaven preserve them!

MAN 2. What a sea it is!

DAVID. I've been in Yarmouth when it blew great guns, but I have never seen the like of this. What are you men doing here?

MAN 1. There's a ship out there, sir.

MAN 2. A schooner, sir. A little foreign schooner being broken, broadside on, by the waves.

MAN 1. Oh, God, look!

The bed has become the ship in the distance. A MAN climbs up and waves from the highest point.

DAVID. An awful sight: to watch men die and be helpless to prevent it.

MAN 2. There's a man still at the masthead.

Enter HAM.

HAM. Come, shipmates. There's still a chance to save him.

HAM strips to the waist and ties a rope about his middle.

DAVID. Ham! Ham! Stop! Are you insane? Look at the sea. There is nothing you can do to save that man. You will merely add your own death to his.

HAM. Master Davy? Is that you under that coat?

DAVID. Ham! For the love of God, Ham, what are you doing? Trying to kill yourself?

HAM. No such thing. I'm trying to save a poor soul as is clinging like a limpet to the mast of that foundering craft. If I gets to it afore it breaks to pieces, I reckon there's a chance we'll live to tell the tale.

DAVID. You cannot go. (*To the others*.) You cannot let him do this! It is plain suicide!

HAM. Davy, bor! Be easy, now. If my time has come, 'tis come. If it ain't, I'll bide it. Come, mates, make ready!

HAM dives into the sea. He reaches the ship, hauls himself up on the deck and reaches out for the MAN at the mast. Just as they touch the storm takes the boat, and they are lost. The storm dies down. The bed taken apart, moved off. Two ruined bodies are laid down, roughly covered with blankets. DAVID looks disbelievingly at HAM's corpse.

DAVID. Oh, God! Ham! Is this my friend?

MAN 1. Yes, sir... And this is the man he was trying to save.

He pulls the blanket from the face of the other body. It is STEERFORTH.

DAVID. Steerforth... Oh, Ham. Ham, my silent, true and honourable friend. You have died – for Steerforth.

Scene Forty-One

DAVID. Lost. Darkness before my eyes. As a man upon a battlefield will receive a mortal hurt, and scarcely know that he is struck, so I, when left alone, had no conception of the wound with which I had to strive. I went away from the coasts of England, and tried to lose myself in other lands – France, Switzerland, and Italy. Alone amongst the stillness of the mountains, the peace – the serenity of nature, spoke to me, awakened some long-forgotten sense of beauty in my breast. I began to weep. Once commenced, I wept as I had not done since Dora died, and doing so, found the clear, quiet spirit of the mountainside had seeped into my heart and soothed its ache. A letter came from Agnes.

AGNES. My dearest David, I give you no advice, I urge no duty on you. I know that in the end you will turn affliction to good. I know that you will labour on, that you will find in your sorrow, your strength. I commend you to God, and assure you that my affection will cherish you always, and is always by your side wherever you may be.

DAVID. Agnes. I have been sore in need of that letter. Oh, Agnes, my beloved friend. The night is passing from my mind. My grief shall not overwhelm me. Rather shall I make it the well-spring of a worthy future... I began to write. A story grew.

The CHARACTERS *from the story gather round* DAVID.

STEERFORTH. Young Copperfield? You shall be our chief storyteller.

HAM. Come on, Master Davy, we'll stow your gear, and Emily and me will show you round.

DORA. Mr Copperfield, my little dog Jip has run off. Would you help me look for him? I think he may be in the shrubbery.

PEGGOTTY. And my Davy became a man.

DICK. A new name goes with a new life.

BETSEY. We shall make our young David a proper gentleman. What do you think of that?

DAVID. My book was published, and I acquired a reputation as an author. Months lengthened into years; and I grew into an established and successful novelist. Agnes wrote to me of her pride in my achievement. I wrote to her that it was she who had inspired me. Agnes. I cannot say at what time I began to think of Agnes. Had I declared her my sister and in my innocence sacrificed – what? What sacrifice had I required Agnes to make? What could I do now, to cancel the mistakes of the past? And might this present be yet another error? If I am now mistaken, if I betray feelings that are not returned in equal measure, I shall have set a wall between us that I can never breach. I cannot take such a risk. Agnes will never be mine. But I will not banish myself for ever from her side. It is time to go home.

Scene Forty-Two

Dover. The bed is pushed on. BETSEY *makes it up with sheets and blankets.* DAVID *is watching* DICK *with an enormous kite.*

BETSEY. Well, David, do you find us much changed?

DAVID. Only that you wear spectacles now, Aunt.

BETSEY. Mr Wickfield you will find much changed. A white-haired old man, though a better man. A reclaimed man.

DAVID. The influence of Agnes?

BETSEY. When are you going to see them? You will find her as good, as beautiful, as earnest, as she has always been.

DAVID. Has Agnes any –

BETSEY. Any what?

DAVID. Any... lover, Aunt.

BETSEY. A score. She might have married twenty times, my dear, since you have been gone.

DAVID. But she hasn't?

BETSEY. I suspect she has one particular attachment, David.

DICK. Definitely. A particular attachment. I think she should marry.

BETSEY. We must not be ruled by suspicions, Mr Dick. We have no right to speak. Come.

BETSEY *and* DICK *exit.*

DAVID. No doubt she will tell me.

Scene Forty-Three

AGNES *comes on.*

AGNES. Tell you what, David?

DAVID. Dear Agnes! The happiness it is to me, to see you once again!

AGNES. And I rejoice to see you, my famous author! You must tell me what it is like to be so grand.

    DAVID *turns and speaks out front, away from her. He is panicking.*

DAVID. So true, so beautiful, so good. So dear to me! I try to bless you, to thank you, to tell you of your influence on me – damn it! To say I love you! And I am struck dumb! (*To* AGNES.) Tell me what has been happening to you.

AGNES. Papa is well. Our anxieties are at rest, our home is restored to us. I teach my girls, we live quietly. And knowing that, you know all.

DAVID. 'All'? There is nothing else? Sister?

AGNES. David –

DAVID. Yes?

AGNES. Will you stay in England now, or do you intend to go abroad again?

DAVID. What does my sister say to my going abroad?

AGNES. I hope you do not.

DAVID. Then I have no such intention.

AGNES. I am so pleased.

DAVID. And I am pleased to hear you say so.

AGNES. Your growing reputation and success enlarge your power of doing good. If I *could* spare my brother, perhaps the time could not.

DAVID *strides away from her, and is met by* BETSEY *and* DICK. AGNES *fades into background.*

Scene Forty-Four

BETSEY. Well, child?

DAVID. Mr Wickfield and Agnes send their good regards to you both. I have some work to do, Aunt. Forgive me if I retire to my books.

DICK. I never thought when I read books, what work it was to write them.

DAVID. It's work enough to read them, sometimes. As to the writing, it has its own charms, Mr Dick.

BETSEY. You remind me, David, someone has written to you. (*She produces a letter.*) I must tell you, I have confirmed an impression. About Agnes, and the attachment I spoke of.

DAVID. Yes?

DICK. We think Agnes is going to be married.

DAVID. Then – God bless her.

BETSEY. God bless her, and her husband too. Now read your letter. (*She goes.*)

DAVID. God bless you, Agnes, for I have lost you. (*He looks at the letter.*) Why, this is from Micawber!

Scene Forty-Five

Enter MICAWBER, *now very grand, and exotically dressed, as if for the tropics.*

MICAWBER. My Dear Sir: Years have elapsed since I have had an opportunity of ocularly perusing those lineaments, now familiar to the imaginations of a considerable portion of the civilised world. But though estranged by the force of circumstances and of a distance over which I have no control, I have not been unmindful of your soaring flight. You must go on! Go on, my dear sir, on your eagle's course! Among the eyes elevated towards you from this far portion of the globe, will ever be found, while it has light and life, the eye appertaining to Wilkins Micawber, *Magistrate*.

DAVID. *Magistrate?* Oh, Micawber, you hero! You Quixote, you Ali Baba! A magistrate! What can I do but obey such an eloquent appeal? I will go on, sir. I will go on!

Scene Forty-Six

Enter AGNES, *who sits on the edge of the bed.* DAVID *runs to* AGNES. *He sits beside her.*

DAVID. My dear Agnes, do you doubt my being true to you?

AGNES. No, of course not.

DAVID. Do you doubt my being what I always have been to you?

AGNES. No.

DAVID. I tried to tell you, when I came home first, what a debt of gratitude I owed you, and – and how fervently I felt towards you.

AGNES. 'Fervently'? David, I –

DAVID. Agnes! I went away from England in my grief, dear
   Agnes, loving you as my sister. I stayed away, loving you. I
   have come home loving you.

AGNES. As I have loved you, David.

DAVID. As my sister?

AGNES. No, David. I told you once before – I am not your
   sister, and you should not think of me so.

DAVID. I know that now. Agnes – if you love me, as I love you
   – not as sister – will you love me in the future as your
   husband? For I most assuredly wish to love you as my wife.

AGNES. Only if you will hear one thing which I must say.

DAVID. What is it?

AGNES. David Copperfield – I have loved you all my life.

A pause. DAVID *stares at* AGNES. *A smile grows on his
face, and at length, they embrace. Fade to black.*

The End.